Archaeologically yours, Beatrice Sandelowsky

*A personal journey into the prehistory of
Southern Africa,
in particular Namibia*

For
Ayanda, Rejoice, Liam and Charmaine
and for
Shakira Beatrice

ISBN 99916-40-57-6

Cover design: Heike Lorck

Cover photo: Beatrice Sandelowsky: Excavating the stone cairn at Gorob River
                Mouth, Kuiseb River

Illustrations: Beatrice Sandelowsky unless specified

Published by: Namibia Scientific Society
                P. O. Box 67
                Windhoek
                NAMIBIA

Printed by: John Meinert Printing, Windhoek, Namibia

FOREWORD

It has been a pleasure for me to know a number of archaeologists in Africa, who have devoted their lives to the documentation of our human heritage through meticulous excavations and research. Among these is Beatrice Sandelowsky, who, however, is unique in that she has had a second life-long passion - that of improving the prospects of indigenous people, particularly in her beloved Namibia, and of drawing their attention to the richness and importance of their own ancient heritage. Beatrice is, by nature, a people's person, primarily concerned with the well-being of her fellow humans, irrespective of their tribal origin or background. Perhaps this concern stems from the fact that she is very social by nature and spent her early years on a farm bordering the Namib Desert. Here her playmates were Damara children, whose company meant a great deal to her and with whom she conversed in their own language.

For her doctoral work in archaeology, Beatrice was fortunate to have had the encouragement and supervision of three of Africa's best-known archaeologists, Desmond Clark, Glynn Isaac and Brian Fagan, at the University of California's Berkeley campus. But coming back to southern Africa in the mid-nineteen-sixties, at the height of the apartheid era regime, it was inevitable that someone as liberal-minded as Beatrice, would have been viewed with suspicion, not only in Windhoek, but also at the University of the Western Cape where she lectured, but where long-term career opportunities were denied her. However, Beatrice was not the sort of person to simply accept any intolerable situation as she found it. Back in Windhoek during 1978, she enlisted the help of some of her friends, drew on her life's savings of one thousand Rand and a Leakey Foundation grant of 175 dollars and founded The University Centre for Studies in Namibia, or TUCSIN, that aimed to enable Namibians from difficult backgrounds to prepare themselves for tertiary education and for their future careers. These TUCSIN programmes have been highly successful - for instance, the Complementary Course, preparing people for tertiary training in natural science fields, has been attended by about 2000 students, while almost 500 have benefitted from TUCSIN-administered scholarships at universities and technikons. For instance, the Deutsche Akademische Austauschdienst alone has funded over 700 student-years of study through TUCSIN.

Apart from this kind of practical contribution that Beatrice and her supportive colleagues have made to education in Namibia, ordinary people have also been encouraged to regain their dignity by learning of their age-old heritage through archaeology. A good deal of Beatrice's field work has focussed on Iron Age sites where indigenous people smelted metals for hundreds of years. Such furnaces have pipes, or tuyères, leading into them, through which air is blown from hand-pumped bellows. Throughout Africa, such pipes have typically been made of clay, but early on in her career, Beatrice discovered that ancient Namibian tuyères had been carved from soapstone, indicating an exclusively local tradition, which also extended to their non-bantu style pottery. She excavated an old smelting site close to the town of Rehoboth, south of Windhoek, and decided that the local Damara and Nama people, who had contributed to the Baster community there, should be made aware of the ancient traditions practised by their ancestors. With the help of her friends and some colleagues from TUCSIN, she started the Rehoboth Museum, housing it initially in the disused house of Rehoboth's first postmaster there. This was the first museum to be established in a non-white Namibian community and has since grown into an important educational facility. The fact that the local people now want complete control over its management suggests that their social pride is starting to re-emerge.

The career and concerns of Beatrice Sandelowsky, brought to life so well in this book, remind one of how much can be done with very little money, but with an abundance of enthusiasm. And her enthusiasm has always been highly infectious, spreading among a wide spectrum of her friends and associates. This meant that if she needed help with a project, whether it involved travelling to some inaccessible cave, excavating a hearth, building a museum display, or organising an educational course, there were always willing helpers at hand. Some of these will have been social friends, others, grateful people that she herself had helped with the promotion of their own careers. They were all caught up in the excitement of her approach to life, which she has also managed to convey so well in this highly unusual book. I recommend it without reservation to anyone interested in the people of southern Africa and their ancient heritage.

C. K. (Bob) Brain
Emeritus Curator at the Transvaal Museum,
Pretoria, South Africa

ACKNOWLEDGEMENTS

When my friends, Karin Lubisch and Sally Frankental, read the first parts of this book written thirty years ago, they thought it was great. The only publisher to whom I submitted the material felt I was too young to write that sort of thing. In the nineties Dr Wolfram Hartman, UNAM, wanted to reprint a series of articles I had published over the years and suggested tying them together against the background of some personal anecdotes. His enthusiasm on reading what I had written long ago encouraged me to go on writing. I was able to do this after my retirement from TUCSIN but not without the care and loyal support of my partner, Wend Ewest.

The encouragement of Bob Brain, Megan Biesele and Lynette Lang was crucial for continuing with a task which became larger than planned. Then Wolfram told me that Herman van Wyk of Gamsberg Macmillan Publishers wanted to publish the book. Many friends and colleagues were eager to help and they promoted the project: Duncan Miller contributed special information and Wade Pendleton sent photographs. Hans Scholz read the manuscript and gave valuable advice. Ursula Mussgnug, Henriette Rispel, Goodman Gwasira, Oliver and Julie Lubisch, Ismael Katjitae, Adolf Denk and Gerdis Stadtherr read the manuscript in parts or as a whole and made important comments. Professor Jekura Kavari spent several hours unselfishly perusing and correcting the text of the Omutandu for cattle. Wend and his sister, Marion Rockstrohen, patiently listened for hours to my reading out aloud the final chapters as one more exercise of editing this work.

Sadly, many persons whom I would have liked to read this book are no longer around. *In absentia* I do want to record my appreciation for the vital role they played in my life. In particular I pay tribute to Professor Desmond Clark and to Keith Robinson who so confidently inspired me to do research in southern Africa. I owe an even greater debt to my cousin, Dr Ursula Arnsdorff who enabled me to come to the USA to pursue my studies at the University of Rochester, New York and at the University of California in Berkeley.

I sincerely thank all those whom I mentioned and who may enjoy reading this book, for their friendship that enriched my life.

Beatrice Sandelowsky

Windhoek
August 2004

Contents

Chapter 8

Chapter 9

Chapter 10

Chapter 11

Chapter 12

CHAPTER 1

A RESEARCH EXPEDITION TO MALAWI

The thought of being invited to join an expedition with internationally famous scientists, had a dreamlike quality for me when I was a graduate student of archaeology at the University of California in Berkeley in the mid sixties. Professor Desmond Clark, doyen of African Prehistory, was planning to do fieldwork in Malawi.

I remember a mild surprise every now and then when I would remind myself that basic things like sleeping, eating and dressing were still part of life. They struck me as the only links with the way of life I was accustomed to. My everyday life in Sout West Africa as a child and later, as a teacher had centred on enabling one to continue dressing, eating and sleeping. At university in America these matters had become subsidiary and were merely necessary to continue with the *real* thing.

Professor Desmond Clark and his wife Betty on 28 February 1985 when he received an Honorary Doctorate from the University of the Witwatersrand (Photo C.K. Brain)

This real thing was the study of the human being and its behaviour, more particularly - past behaviour - for the student of palaeo-anthropology or archaeology. It took me a while to get used to the fact that showing an interest in the things I had been taught to consider 'unimportant' was no longer deemed ridiculous or a waste of time. When my father took me along on drives through the veld on our Namib-farm and I was begging to stop so that I could have a closer look at a certain flower or pick up a stone the response used to be... "My dear child, there is no time." And when I nagged the only comfort was: "You will come back to this place many, many times and *then* there may be time to stop and

1

look." Now there was a prize on noticing things others had not noticed, on asking questions for which there were no ready answers or of which others had not thought.

Our house on the Namib-farm Nordenburg

The team going to Malawi in July 1966 was led by Professor Clark and his wife, Betty, and included John Ogbu, Laurel Lofgren and myself as graduate students. John Yellen would join us later in the season. Also included were Sonia Cole, well-known for books she had written on the prehistory of East Africa and Glen Cole (not related to Sonia) from the Field Museum in Chicago and Vance Haynes, a well-known geologist were also part of our group.

I was burning to please, to be considered acceptable and to make a favourable impression. There was no task I would not have leapt to and none that I felt too difficult to handle. I scaled the top of the high five ton truck not understanding why the others were surprised. Admittedly, there was not much competition that morning when we were packing and my height and physical fitness stood me in good stead. Laurel was about half my size, and John Ogbu, from a noble family in Nigeria, was the epitome of the absent-minded professor with little aptitude for solving practical tasks.

We set off from Blantyre in three vehicles and drove to Karonga on the northern edge of Lake Malawi. The streets of the village were decorated with colourful little flags and banners bearing inscriptions such as 'REPUBLIC DAY 6TH July 1966' in anticipation of President Banda's first visit to these areas.

There were uniformed young men riding around in Land Rovers labelled MALAWI CONGRESS PARTY, instilling curiosity and excitement. Malawi was celebrating its second year of Independence after colonial British rule in 1966.

Banners decorated the streets of Karonga on Republic Day: 6 July 1966

Young men in smart uniforms were driving Land Rovers of the MALAWI CONGRESS PARTY

Our camp was pitched a few kilometres outside Karonga on flat terrain of bush country. A grass wall enclosure around a huge Jacaranda tree provided a communal area where we shared our meals around a large table where finds were sorted, maps were drawn or studied and what social life there was, took place. Around this central enclosure called 'banda', tents were pitched in the places where the shade of the trees would fall during the hottest part of the day. Compared with my previous camping experience, this was a

Sonia Cole was walking across fossiliferous formations, looking for traces of early humans

luxurious affair. The tents were huge and each one was equipped with stretcher, sleeping bag, table, chair and canvas wash-basin and bath! I cannot remember any other bathroom, which I appreciated - and enjoyed - as much as I did this one.

The tent did not, however, contain a toilet. This was another sophisticated affair by my standards. It consisted of a pit known as a Long Drop, which had a clay mound fitted with a toilet seat constructed on top of it. Two steps carved into the clay led to the throne, which was flanked by spacious platforms useful for paper, reading matter and small luggage. I managed to get a laugh out of Betty Clark because I had furnished the place with an in-flight-magazine from Air Malawi entitled "Welcome Aboard."

The first few days of our stay were spent relocating sites that had been worked the previous year and different members of the team adopted individual projects. I was still too overawed by the whole undertaking to even consider taking charge of a site by myself. So I worked for short periods at different sites, helping out where needed. Mainly I attached myself to Sonia Cole who was walking over fossiliferous formations looking for traces of early humans and their occupation sites.

MWANGANDA'S SITE

Eventually we concentrated our efforts on a site not far from the lake shore where the bones of at least one elephant had been discovered near Mwanganda's village. We were dropped off there at 06:30 every morning with three or four local assistants and fetched again at three or four in the afternoon. Most of the hours were spent jamming the sharp ends of tooth probes into the hard calcareous matrix embedding the fossil bone, while the blunt ends gradually penetrated the palms of our hands. Only occasionally was this work interrupted by taking a photographic record of our progress or drawing a plan or section of an area that was exposed. The roughly worked stone tools that were found in association with the bones enhanced the interest of this site.

Professor Clark estimated that the site we were excavating dated back to the Upper Pleistocene or the beginning of the Middle Stone Age. How amazing to think that here we were in touch – literally – with a scene, which was staged perhaps as long as 150,000 years ago. I tried to imagine the actors of the time. Would they have been fully human as we are? Perhaps they did not even have language as we have. But they had been organised enough to subdue an animal as large as a hippo or an elephant and they had been able to dismember the huge carcass with no more than stone flakes – not even the equivalent of pocket knives!

Nevertheless, these regularly shaped flakes which we were finding implied learning behaviour and begged the question of tool making versus tool using. Birds dropping clam shells on rocks to open them up are using the rocks as tools. They cannot make tools because they have no hands, but would they be able to if they had hands?! What is it that distinguishes us from other animals? Does it all have to do with that many-splendoured brain power we believe we have?

According to the implements we were finding, it would appear that this was a butcher site only and not a place where people were staying permanently. As far as we could make out, the bones we were finding belonged to a single animal only and this supported the idea of a large kill being consumed or divided up on the spot rather than the enormous mass of meat being transported back to the place of the household.

While I am writing this, Professor Clark's book, published in 1971, is lying next to me open to the page where he discusses Mwanganda's site. It provides a wonderful feeling of satisfaction to see how the work we did there was used and related to a larger body of knowledge which contributed to an understanding of how human behaviour evolved.

The hours of almost solitary work at Mwanganda's village site allowed a great deal of time for thinking. I remembered events, that led to me being where I was. The inauguration of the Namib Desert Research Station, Gobabeb, in 1963 had been a significant experience. Dr. Charles Koch, the founder of the Station, was a charming Austrian entomologist who had discovered the amazing adaptations of protein conversion in tenebrionid beetles, commonly called 'toktokkies'. He assumed that such adaptation must have taken a very long time to develop and consequently dubbed the Namib "the oldest desert in the world". His young assistant, Wulf Haacke, made an even greater impression on me. He was a herpetologist at the Transvaal Museum in Pretoria and was the star of the day because he had only a day before discovered the Golden Mole *(Eremitalpa granti)* in the sand dunes. For a long time this small mammal had been considered extinct.

Not long after this momentous contact with people in the world of scientific research, Rona MacCalman, archaeologist at the State Museum in Windhoek, suggested that I request a transfer from the school in Swakopmund where I was a teacher to the State Museum in Windhoek. By the beginning of 1964 Dr. Willem Steyn, then Director of the Museum, ably handled this happy switch and I was assigned to be Rona MacCalman's assistant. Dr. Steyn was another dedicated herpetologist. When he made his rounds at the museum it would not be unusual for him to pull one or other reptile out of the pocket of his white lab coat and explain the unique arrangement of scales on the creature's body or another eye that had been discovered on some rare lizard.

At weekly staff meetings over a cup of tea, turns were taken to report on the work one was busy with at the time. I was inspired and thrilled to work in such an atmosphere and very ambivalent about giving up my position when my cousin invited me to go to the United States of America for a year for further studies. But upon Dr. Steyn's encouragement "....you go and get your Ph.D. and together we shall then make this museum famous...." I took up the opportunity of doing full time studies in Anthropology in the United States. Rona, who had graduated from Cambridge under the supervision of Professor Desmond Clark, encouraged me to link up with him at the University of California in Berkeley........

Evenings and weekends at the Karonga camp were marked by glorious dips in the tepid waters of Lake Malawi. By now my enchantment with scientific work had worn off sufficiently to allow me to scheme to be allowed to take a vehicle and drive the approximately ten kilometres to the shore, although I did feel guilty about taking off for sheer pleasure. Occasionally Sonia would join me and make me feel better about the little venture. She was a most likeable, handsome woman who had worked in East Africa for many years. She talked about Louis and Mary Leakey, who had become famous with their finds of human ancestors in the Rift Valley of Kenya, as though they were ordinary people. That was something, which from my perspective seemed unlikely and I was thrilled at having the privilege of association in this way.

The composition of our team changed from time to time. Some team members left and new people arrived. Keith Robinson was a familiar name from his many papers in the scientific journal 'Arnoldia', published in Rhodesia and from the South African Archaeological Bulletin. He was an old friend of the Clarks and they were looking forward to his arrival. He was the Iron Age specialist and I was interested in the transition of the Later Stone Age to the Iron Age. If the descendents of the almost human people who had killed the elephant at Mwanganda's site had evolved into biologically modern *Homo Sapiens* 150 or 120 thousand years ago they would have continued to live as hunter-gatherers for some one hundred thousand years before pottery and iron came into use. That had happened only some two thousand years ago in southern Africa. That historic transition fascinated me.
"What sort of person is Keith Robinson?" I ventured at dinner one evening.
"A very strange man. A loner who does not like women," was the unambiguous answer given by Betty Clark.
I immediately regretted being a woman. I would have considered a sex change if that would have qualified me to work with Keith Robinson on the Iron Age. When Professor Clark suggested that Laurel and I go up and work on the Nyika Plateau my feelings were a bit mixed because Laurel and I did not agree on a number of things. Consequently I felt rather dejected.

The day Keith arrived we had chocolate mousse for dessert and I thought how incongruous it was to welcome a loner and a woman-hater with a dish like that. Then I found out that he also was a teetotaller. It took me days to gather up enough courage to go and speak to him whilst he was washing the potsherds he had found that day. He only glanced at me once or twice but he did talk, explaining the differences in the patterns that were mostly on the rims of the sherds. That evening the trip to the Nyika was again brought up. I was completely taken aback when Laurel said that she had decided against going up and wanted to leave the expedition when she had finished the work at her present site.
"How do you feel about going up to the Nyika alone, Beatrice?" Professor Clark asked me.

Without thinking I said:

"I'll go."

"I don't think I can let you have a car all to yourself, but we'll take you up there and then you can get porters."

There was silence around the table and I thought I must say something otherwise someone might say that it could not be done.

"I'm sure that will be no problem, I must only find someone to show me where Fingira Hill is situated on the Nyika Plateau", I heard myself saying and Clark replied:

"That's no problem. You can see that from far away. It is a very conspicuous granite dome and if you approach it from the south- east you cannot miss the shelter."

Then he described the paintings and some of the artefacts he had found on the surface of the shelter's floor. I had trouble concentrating because I kept thinking that I could really go. He really meant it. He would not be discussing this with me if he did not want to let me go.

The next day when we were again pushing our tooth probes into our hands and the elephant deposit, Sonia Cole asked me whether I was not worried about going up to the Nyika without a car. Only then did I really consider the implications of my temerity. Betty had said earlier that it was typical of Desmond to make such a suggestion because he was oblivious of the practicalities of sustaining human life in ways other than by looking at fossils and stone tools. I had never been to the area and did not even know how far the nearest settlement would be from my camp. The thing that worried me most was my ignorance of any local language as the Nyika Plateau certainly was an area remote enough to make it unlikely that English would be spoken or even understood by the local population. But at the same time I was grateful to Betty for not having opposed the scheme outright. She had obviously realised how much it meant to me.

As I was sorting out the tools and equipment to take along, I decided to ask Professor Clark whether Masters, one of the assistants with whom I had worked together so far, and who spoke English quite well, could accompany me. I also wanted to work out some point of communication at which a weekly check would be made, to see if I had left any message. How surprised I was when he said:

" Well, that won't be necessary because Keith has decided to go with you, so you can keep the car. Masters can go along as well."

"I beg your pardon?"

"Keith wants to have a look for Iron Age sites on the Nyika and maybe he can help you with the excavation, and you can keep the car."

I had heard correctly but was nevertheless confused. I had been promoted from being in the company of an unenthusiastic fellow student to being the companion of a loner and woman-hater. Perhaps that would be better than going off into the wilderness and isolation with a Don Juan. I steeled myself to have a closer look at my companion-to-be. His tanned, stringy body looked like a stick figure in khaki shorts and bush shirt that seemed too large. His shoulders were slightly hunched over and more often than not one saw the top of his khaki cloth hat rather than his face as he was bending down over his sieve, sorting or cleaning the potsherds. I wanted to get a snapshot of him but did not succeed in doing it unnoticed. When he looked at me as I snapped the camera there was a twinkle in his eye. My heart skipped a few beats as I realised that there was humour and kindness behind this forbidding scrawny façade.

7

A breathtakingly beautiful trip passed through different habitats

UP TO THE NYIKA PLATEAU

It was a day's trip to Chelinda, the game lodge on top of the Nyika Plateau. A breathtakingly beautiful trip, passed through three different habitats separated from one another by two steep drops of appr. 1,300 metres of altitude. When we left Karonga early in the morning, it was oppressively warm and small flies were swarming around the mango

Fingira Hill - a prominent granite dome - could be seen on the horizon

trees. For a short distance we travelled along the lakeshore and then wound ourselves along 22 hairpin curves within eleven kilometres, up to the Livingstonia Plateau. It was cooler here and although banana trees and paw paws still implied tropical conditions, otherwise different vegetation reflected lower temperatures and less humidity than on the more humid, hotter lakeshore.

The afternoon saw another climb up to the Nyika Plateau with rapidly decreasing temperatures. We reached Chelinda at dusk and had the signpost read "Brigadoon" instead of Chelinda, I would not have been surprised. Pine forests stretched down soft slopes to a small, mirror top lake. Picturesque chalets built out of white limestone studded what looked like a green pasture. Chilled to the bone I stepped into the lounge of the chalet we had booked into for the night and there, to greet me, were the most friendly, bright, orange flames crackling in the fireplace. It was difficult to visualise the rest of our team sitting around the table in the Karonga banda absorbing cool drink after cool drink in an effort to combat heat and dehydration.

When I woke up in the morning it was bitterly cold and beneath a heavy blanket of fog there was frost on the ground. I liked the game ranger for saying that Fingira Hill was at a slightly lower altitude than Chelinda and that if we chose a sheltered spot we had a chance of survival. I trusted him but borrowed a blanket to improve the chances. Fingira Hill - with 'our' shelter - was on the day's programme and as the fog lifted, a prominent granite dome could be seen on the horizon. But there was some rough country between that point and us. We followed a road leading in that general direction which ended in a schoolyard. Some very friendly teachers, who had talked to Dr Clark as well, met us. They could help us with our requests for guides and porters and within less than half an hour we were on our way in single file on a narrow path down steep valleys and up again. There were flatter areas but then again steep slopes. On that first day the shelter seemed to be at the very top of an incredibly high and steep mountain. Completely exhausted I leaned against a rock and tried to take in the rock paintings and the whole appearance of the ancient occupation site.

Large geometric designs in red and white were badly weathered, but nevertheless communicated a rhythm and a sense of completeness (computer generated image - actual size 1,25m across)

9

The large geometric designs in red and white were indeed badly weathered but neverthe-less communicated a rhythm and a sense of being complete which I never tired of looking at. When had this painting been made? In contrast to the representational rock art of animals and people in Namibia, this curvaceous red and white composition could only be identified as symbolic. This was the work of modern human beings, possibly done as recently as one or two thousand years ago. This was the Later Stone Age – it surged through my mind. And Keith would go and find an Iron Age site …. I was fantasizing.

FINGIRA HILL ROCK SHELTER

We set up our camp on the site of a recently deserted homestead at the head of a valley fed by a spring. A few steps from where the front door used to be, soft crystal-clear water was gently bubbling out of the ground amidst a patch of particularly lush vegetation. The endless variety of exquisitely flowering shrubs, the thick carpet of juicy green grass, ferns and patches of cedar forest gave my image of Africa a new dimension, worlds apart from my own dry desert home.

Keith Robinson sitting inside our banda attached to the wall of an old mud house

We had visitors from nearby villages who brought such local products as clay pots, onions, millet and honey. There was honey in bark dishes, honey in old tins, honey in clay pots and enamel mugs. I believe the healthy climate and all this honey overcame an initial bout of kidney trouble and diarrhoea that had troubled me during the first few days. The Sunday after our arrival, when Keith wanted to go to Chelinda to send a message to Professor Clark that we were alive and well, I decided to stay in camp. In fact I stayed in bed most of the day and got up only to fetch new supplies of tea, water and honey. I said to myself that depending on how I felt that evening, I would decide on whether to tell Keith about my problems or not. Although we were by now talking to each other there was still some considerable social distance between us.

"No, Beatrice, I don't think I will forget your name" (Photo K. Robinson)

That evening, absorbing the warmth of our little cooking fire inside the banda we had built onto one of the walls of the old homestead, we discussed some books and papers that he was going to send me. As I was handing him back the notebook into which I had written my address, I realised that I had not put my name above it and I said, "Oh, my name, Keith will you remember that?" I seriously thought that it would be quite understandable if a great scientist soon forgot the name of such an insignificant person as myself. But he laughed and said, "No, Beatrice, I don't think I'll forget your name."

Again there was that twinkle in his eye and an unsuccessful attempt at suppressing great amusement at my naivety. The misogynistic attitude seemed to be disintegrating. As the days passed I found it easier and easier to get up early in the morning. The walk to the site shrunk in time and distance and I wasn't even out of breath when we reached the shelter. By leaping from one familiar rock to the next, I now easily crossed places that had taken me three to four calculated steps at our first ascent. Our trench, initially five metres long and one metre across, was gradually gaining in depth and yielded an enormous number of finds. Masters had instructed the local team of five workers very efficiently and was continually ensuring that they be "pachoko - pachoko" - very, very careful. So we were brushing thin layers of the ashy, dusty deposit into small piles in the centre of each square metre of our grid. These little heaps were then brushed into buckets, which in turn were emptied into sieves with a mesh small enough to retain tiny ostrich eggshell beads. The fine dust that resulted from this procedure is hard to describe. It penetrated the skin, and particularly the fingertips, which became hard, with the skin cracking in places and taking on a dark grey colour with black veins, which it took weeks to clean.

Most of our time was spent sorting through the sieves, picking out stone tools, bone fragments and pieces of ostrich eggshell. "Typical Later Stone Age assemblage," Keith remarked.

The view from the shelter was magnificent. On clear days we could make out Lake Malawi glistening in the distance.

Every grid square had its own set of paper bags, which were closed up and labelled, whenever we had gone through another five centimetre thick layer. I remember watching one of the men pouring yet another bucket into the sieve and seeing the loose earth falling away from the larger items. One item seemed particularly large and Keith, who was standing behind me, literally made a dive for it. He quickly turned it from side to side, rubbed it between the palms of his hands and a little breathlessly, said:
"Will you look at that?"
It was a flat, oval, black stone axe, carefully worked on both sides, with one edge ground smooth from usage. It was a dark fine-grained rock and I thought it was beautiful.
"Is that an axe, Keith?"
"Yes, and a very nice one. Desmond used to think that axes and bored stones are typical for Malawi but when you start looking for them, they are not all that easy to find."

Who made the very first axe of this kind? And why? This must have been invention rather than discovery. I had taken a course on 'Invention and Discovery'. However brilliant an invention might have been, history told us, it needed to be accepted by the society unless it would simply be forgotten. Many significant inventions and discoveries had been made more than once before their importance was generally recognised. The wheel – for instance – and probably also writing - had been invented more than once, in different places and societies.

The stone axe made our day. In very high spirits we were trying to imagine how pleased Desmond Clark would be when he saw it. We started to talk about how we would welcome the Clarks when they came to visit us in a couple of weeks' time. Keith suggested that we make a special dish into which to insert the axe and serve it to Desmond like that. We did, in fact, have a very festive little lunch party for our guests when they came but we did not serve the axe.

One of the things that motivated my getting up at the crack of dawn each day was the fact that the sun shone into the shelter only very early in the mornings. So I was contentedly crouching in my square one morning carefully brushing away the loose, dry, ashy cave earth with a broad paintbrush when something white appeared. Back and forth I brushed a few more times so that I could see more clearly. It was long and narrow. Probably another bone. Don't pick it up, expose it completely - I recited my lesson. There was another one. That's interesting. Lying close to the first one. Slightly faster movement of the brush. No, this definitely is another piece of bone with the same long narrow shape. What bone could this be? Wait a minute, there was yet another one, similarly orientated to the first two.

"Keith! Come and have a look at this lot." As always, he was there in a flash.

"Bones, Beatrice. And I think they are rib bones."

"Of what, do you think?"

"That I don't know. Probably a cow."

"*A cow*??!! A foot below the surface in a pure Later Stone Age deposit?!" I exclaimed.

I was not even sure there were cows anywhere in Africa at that time. If this was another example of Keith Robinson's humour, I did not know whether I was crazy about it, I thought to myself. Perhaps he sensed my slight annoyance because he said:

"Beatrice, don't be careless now. For a young student like yourself it would be an excellent exercise to unearth the articulated skeleton of any animal." Was this even more sarcasm?

But every few minutes he came to look over my shoulder. And they were indeed rib bones. More were appearing. I had to start taking away the loose material that had been brushed aside so that I could lower the surface of the whole square evenly, or else one would start digging an untidy hole and it would be impossible to see whether there were other items associated with these rib bones.

"You know, they might still be attached to the spine. But what a strange orientation they have. It is unusual to come across the bones of the ribs as the first and highest-lying ones if the other skeletal bones still are in position."

"Do you still think they are the bones of a cow?"

"No, I think they are a little too small for that."

Now Keith was starting to lower the surface of the adjacent square. He seemed to be more interested than I would have expected him to be in the bones of an animal.

"Beatrice, there is more bone here!" A fairly agitated voice.

"So what?" I countered, trying to keep my cool.

"Oh, come on now. Those rib bones could be human. I just don't understand why we didn't find a skull first."

"Human? But didn't you say that one never found human bones in rock shelters?"

"I said that unfortunately human skeletons had hardly ever been found in the rock shelters of South Africa, or Rhodesia or elsewhere in Africa for that matter. But one always hopes to find them, anyway."

"Have you found skeletons in shelters before?"

"No. And I have dug in many a shelter."

"But Desmond found two skeletons at Hora Mountain," I interjected.

"That's right," Keith continued.

" And it was a very spectacular discovery. But one needs more material to compare them with. Particularly Later Stone Age material. Probably these people, who may have been living in caves and rock shelters more commonly than their predecessors did not like the idea of keeping their dead in their homes."

"Later Stone Age people would have had well-developed burial practices," I ventured.

"Quite. Maybe they burnt their dead, like the American Indians."
"Do you really think so?" I had not even heard about that ancient ritual.
"No, not really. It's only so hard to understand why one finds so few skeletal remains."
"Perhaps they didn't bury them very well, or not at all. Animals would come and disperse the bones."

The loose material I brushed away from the bones accumulated so fast, I now asked Masters to come and help me take it away, so that I could continue with exposing the bones. Keith had also enlisted the help of one more worker. We were rushing back and forth from the sieve to the square trying to keep up with all the processes simultaneously. On the boundary between the two squares in which we were working, a large rock was starting to emerge. It was large enough to look like bedrock. However, we would have expected bedrock a lot deeper than this. As it turned out later there were a number of huge boulders close to the entrance of the shelter and the deposit filled a large hollow between them and the back wall. The rib cage and a few vertebrae of the spinal cord were lying almost parallel to the edge of the large rock, sloping down in such a way that the body of the person must have been lying head downwards with the legs on higher rocks almost like someone falling down a staircase. We were working feverishly, exposing the bones, but not moving them, taking photographs, drawing plans and all along continuing with the sifting and sorting at the sieves. I remember noticing a bit of dryness in my throat a couple of times and finally saying:
"I really think we should break for tea. It must be well past ten o'clock."
As I looked to see where the shadows were I could not quite believe what I saw and checked my watch. It was four in the afternoon. I was panic-stricken.
"What are we going to do? We won't be able to finish!"
"We could always come back tomorrow."
It was time for some light relief.
"Do you think we should? But what about the bones? Do we just leave them?"
"Let's cover up the trench with some poles and brushwork. I only wonder whether our helpers have realised that we are uncovering a human skeleton."

With Masters' help we asked whether there were any stories or legends connected with this shelter. The Phoka, who were said to be the oldest inhabitants of this area, had used this shelter many years before for rain making ceremonies, we were told. The 'writing on the wall' was attributed to God. Our lack of language proficiency was a crippling handicap. The likelihood of gross misunderstanding was so great that one wondered whether it would not be more accurate to simply acknowledge ignorance. Would it not have been an ideal world if there had been an anthropological linguist amongst us as well? I had taken two fascinating courses in linguistics. That was just enough to make this lack of expertise so painfully clear.

Our brushwork continued early the following day and, to our amazement, we uncovered stones where we were expecting the skull and limbs. They were melon sized rocks and, as I was blowing away the dust around them, I tried to explain their presence to myself.
"Let's photograph them and then we shall just have to lift them. The bones should be lying below the stones".

That was a possibility. The first stone I lifted lay close to a part of the humerus. A great deal of blowing and very light brushing revealed a shattered piece of bone. Hundreds of little splinters and jagged edges. We looked at each other somewhat bewildered.

"This stone must have come to rest here with considerable force," Keith observed. "But I' m surprised that all the little splinters are still here."

"Yes, that is odd. The only explanation for that is that the bone was still held together by the skin and the flesh when it was broken."

"Do you think this guy was killed by a rock- fall from the roof of the shelter?" was all I could think of.

"I don't know. But this rock seems very small for that and so carefully aimed at the elbow."

"But where is the head?"

"With this being the right arm it can only be right down there next to the big rock."

As I was exposing a little more of the pelvic bones to make sure that the orientation was correct, the edge of another rock appeared below it, leaving just a narrow crevice between two large boulders. The pelvic girdle was slightly angled, almost as though it had been pushed in between the rocks. The surface of the second rock sloped down at a steeper angle than the one closer to the front of the shelter and the body had apparently been lying on this one. We were still missing the head, the left arm, hand and foot bones. I could not bear the idea of not finding the skull and started to move the surrounding soft deposit that prevented my getting into the corner between the two large rocks. Keith's concern was the missing limb.

"Unless they removed the guy's left arm before they buried him it has to be in that little crevice in the rocks there."

"Do you think they tried to push him into that narrow slit in the stones?"

"He must have been squashed against the rock"

"Well, I don't think he grew out of it."

"You're so helpful." I was almost irritated by another sample of that rare Keith Robinson humour.

"I do my best," he replied, obviously highly amused.

Yet another photograph and then I was going to lift the rock that, hopefully, was lying on his face. More blowing and very, very careful brushing.

"Keith, it's here." He was already kneeling next to me.

"He must have been squashed against the rock."

"Oh dear, it's broken." My voice was also breaking.

"We've got glyptol, Beatrice. Just go slowly. We can impregnate the bone with glyptol, which will harden it. Don't worry, we'll manage." There was hardly a trace left of the woman-hater.

I had started looking for the little brush with which to apply the glyptol. We had used it on a fair amount of bone already and there weren't many bristles left on it.

"Do we have another brush at camp?"

"No, we've already gone through two of them."

"What now?"

"Beatrice, my hair is terribly fine, and there isn't much left of it anyway..."

"I know."

With that I started to produce the first in a row of paintbrushes from my long, thick bush of hair. We used them for the treatment of our many bones.

My odd hairstyle intrigued the hairdresser in Blantyre when we got back to town. .....
"Well, you see we had no more paintbrushes.... but there were all those bones. Particularly that lovely skull...that had been smashed by a stone....." Then I shut up because the look on the face of the hairdresser was such a mixture of amazement and fear that I dreaded not getting my hair done....

The breaks in the skull turned out to be fairly clean and most of the crucial features were preserved. The brow was shattered above one eye and the lower jaw was broken between the two front teeth, which had been pushed to lie almost above one another. It must have been a grim burial if not a violent death. What had caused it? Who had been present? When had it happened? The tea break gave me a few moments to linger over those thoughts. Once more the rhythm of the red and white curves on the grey granite wall reached out to me over the depths of time. I tried to imagine an atmosphere of tension, fear and grief, followed by the peace of death.

"Perhaps this was a hide-out during the times of the Nguni raids." Keith's thoughts were along similar lines to mine. Some of the Nguni incursions, which originated in Zululand were said to have been incredibly cruel and the indigenous population is known to have fled from them in anguish. This meant that the deposit was only two to three hundred years old. In that case we should also have found iron and pottery, which we did not.

Soon we could start lifting the bones to examine them. There was no trace of hand or foot bones. Fragments of the left arm were indeed found in the crevice below the shoulder. The leg bones were twisted around the rocks and broken in several places. All the bones were, however, very hard. They were so hard that we thought they could well be semi-fossilised. This impression was verified by the palaeontologist who later examined these Fingira skeletal remains. Apart from that, the skull bone in particular, seemed thick and

The breaks in the skull turned out to be fairly clean. The left eyebrow was shattered and the lower jaw was broken.

robust. From the length of the thigh bones we judged the individual to be of fairly small stature. The teeth were well-worn, so that we assumed them to be those of an adult.

But all these observations had to be investigated much more carefully by specialists so we had to exercise our patience. Similarly we would have to wait at least a few months before our charcoal samples had been dated by carbon 14 analysis for an idea about the age of our finds. Carbon dating had been discovered fairly recently. It was a method of deciding the age of prehistoric organic material by measuring the decay of radio-active carbon 14 in the pieces of charcoal or wood or bone found by archaeologists.

The energy we expended in discovering 'No.1', as we called him, must have been considerable because the reaction was much more subdued when we found 'No 2'. The bones of this skeleton were scattered and consequently required less time and work. But remnants of bone from 14 other skeletons were still to follow! This count was made by Professor Brothwell, a Physical Anthroplogist of the British Museum, who studied every detail of our finds.

We certainly were aware of a great deal of human bone coming to light, and we filled box after box with human bones padded in cotton wool and newspaper. We were working from dawn to dusk in a race against time because I had to get back to California for the beginning of the university term. During those weeks in August and September of 1966 I had thought of very little aside from what concerned my day-to-day life in Malawi. When the news over our small portable short wave radio reported the assassination of South African President Hendrik Verwoerd we talked about the implications for South West Africa, my home country. Who would be the next President? Keith thought Balthasar

Vorster, the Minister of Justice responsible for the South African police at the time, might be considered to succeed Verwoerd. Vorster was rumoured to have had strong ties with fascist regimes of the past and might be even more fanatical than Verwoerd. I did wonder whether the restrictions on foreigners entering the country, let alone applying for permission to do research there, would become even more exacting or whether international pressure would at long last make an impression on the horrendous Apartheid regime. There would be a significant effect on my personal life either way. A serious emotional relationship had developed with Wade Pendleton, a graduate student I had met in the Anthropology Department at Berkeley. He was planning to do urban research in S.W.A./Namibia. Would he be permitted to do that? We had planned to meet in Nairobi and to go back to California via Europe. That was something I had thought about quite often. I was looking forward to the short vacation we had planned to have together in Europe.

Nairobi in the Rift Valley was a Mecca for archaeologists because this was the land of the Leakeys. They had established the Kenya National Museum in Nairobi and had become internationally famous for their discoveries of Early Man in Olduvai Gorge.

There was no time for us to get to Olduvai, but we did visit the Museum and I was trying to imagine what the Windhoek Museum might develop into one day. The city of Nairobi was another fascinating experience, so different from Namibia. Wade pointed out one of the most striking differences: the phenomenon of markets was unknown in Namibia. But here in East Africa buying and selling of all kinds of goods was going on everywhere. We decided that one of the main reasons for this was to be sought in the density of the population. Arid to semi-arid Namibia was one of the least populated countries in the world. At that time - during the mid-sixties - the total population of Namibia was less than a million over an area about the size of Texas. Fertile Kenya was densely populated.

CHAPTER 2

ONCE MORE TO MALAWI

Wade and I spent the next year in Berkeley preparing for the doctoral examination. I was earning money by working on the gazetteer of the *Atlas for African Prehistory*, the 'Bloody Atlas' as it was ambivalently or affectionately referred to in Prof. Clark's office. 'The Atlas of blood and tears' would have been another fitting title.

I was also waiting for the dates from Fingira, the report on the skeletal material and the artefacts from Malawi that I was to analyse. Once the material had been unpacked, there was a non-stop crisis all day and every day until every chip and chunk, flake, core and tool had been recorded as to shapes, lengths, breadths, thicknesses, type of material, type of working applied to the artefact, pattern of scars seen on the surface and various signs of usage. Additional comments were also recorded.

As large sheets of data were filled with the information, which I was going to present and discuss in my doctoral thesis, the question of their security arose. The plan was to return home to Namibia. Should I carry this material with me or should I mail the data to Namibia? The cost of photocopying such large sheets was well beyond my budget limits.

When Professor Clark had asked me whether I wanted to return to Malawi for another field season I had the feeling that my dreams were starting to overtake me. Keith Robinson would join me, to do some more excavations. Wade's proposal to do research in Windhoek had been accepted for funding and he had indeed obtained permission to do his work in SWA/Namibia. We planned a wonderful trip back to Africa via Hawaii, Japan and Thailand. It really was fairytale stuff.

When the day of departure from Berkeley came, I literally did not have time to finish packing my personal belongings. Wade and I were busy packing through the night with friends dropping in all the time. Each one left with either library books to return for us, or with letters to mail or some other errand. Finally it was time to go if we were to catch the plane. I had to close my suitcase and ask my friend, Mike Breger, to please pack the remainder of my things into a box and mail them on.

Our arrival in Malawi did nothing to heal my tattered nerves. Our entire luggage had been lost *en route*. Packed on the bottom of my suitcase there were fifty huge data sheets with the multitude of readings taken from the artefacts of the Fingira excavation. It was awful. I do not know how we managed to survive the three weeks of uncertainty, worry and doubt until the liberating news reached us that the bags had been traced and had been sent on to Blantyre. This wonderful message reached us a day before Wade was due to start on the next lap of his journey to Windhoek. He had a day's stopover in Blantyre and could confirm that the cases had not been opened or tampered with – in other words: the data was safe!

A precious letter from Desmond contained his thoughts on the skeletal remains from Fingira:"…these show that the physical type associated with your Later Stone Age material was short, robustly built and exhibited both Negroid and some Bushmanoid characteristics….." The charcoal samples from Fingira yielded dates of approximately 2400 and 3400 years Before Present.

Keith and I were heading now for our second camp near Rumpi at the base of the Nyika Plateau. The first stop had been Hora Mountain. Here Professor Clark had discovered four rock shelters with human skeletal material in one of them. We located four more rock overhangs and decided to put down test pits in two of them, which were almost adjacent to one another. Rather unimaginatively we labelled them Hora/5 and Hora/7.

Our hopes of finding Iron Age material neatly deposited on top of Later Stone Age material was met in broad terms, but the stratification was far from 'neat' and the finds were sparse in quantity and quality, I thought. I was impatient and unrealistically ambitious at that stage. We could, nevertheless, draw interesting conclusions from comparing the stone artefacts found in these two shelters situated so close to one another.

In the Hora/5 shelter potsherds and metal fragments marked the Iron Age layer in which we also found a few stone artefacts. As we went deeper, more lithic material was found, to the exclusion of pottery and traces of metal. This situation indicated a young date for the Later Stone Age material. Typologically the stone tools resembled the finds from Fingira and other Later Stone Age sites in Malawi. Carbon 14 dates indicated an age of approximately three thousand years.

In the other rock overhang, Hora/7, Iron Age material was found on top of a thick layer of deposit in which we found only isolated artefacts from a Later Stone Age layer.

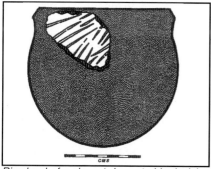

Rimsherd of a claypot decorated by incision found at a depth of 35cm below the surface at Mt Hora/7. The pot outline is not to scale.

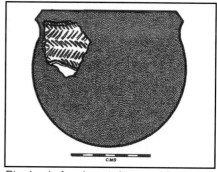

Rimsherd of a claypot decorated by incision found at Hora/7. The pot outline is not to scale.

There was a striking difference between the stone artefacts from the two sites. The radio carbon date giving an age of approximately 14,700 B.C. for the material from the Hora/7 rock shelter highlighted this difference. It indicated that people living long ago had produced stone tools of a much better quality than their descendants thousands of years later.

The stone implements from Hora/5, which resembled the ones from Fingira and other Later Stone Age sites in northern and central Malawi, had been made from a poor quality of white quartz. Their irregular shapes and a poor finish implied a casual work technique and no great demand for skill or standardization. Compared to sites of similar age in southern Africa, the people in Malawi had produced an enormous amount of waste material in the course of making very few well-shaped tools. Only one in every three hundred pieces had been worked into a recognizable stone tool. At other Later Stone Age sites in southern Africa three to ten neatly shaped scrapers, arrow heads, drills or piercers were reported amongst a hundred chips and flakes removed from a larger stone or core. The ancient inhabitants at Hora/7 worked more systematically with their stone material and they were more selective in the choice of their raw material. Although they too worked with quartz they avoided badly fractured pieces and the sugary texture of quartz. Such poor quality raw material was, however, used at Hora/5 and at sites of a similar 'young' age in Malawi.

Diagram of methodically worked core and flakes made of good quality, fine-grained stone: a) a small core showing scars of flakes removed from an "equator" around the edge. b,c & d) flakes showing dorsal sides implying that they had been prepared by previous blows. The ventral sides show regular flake release surfaces.

Two opposing points of view were held about this matter. One opinion maintained that availability of the raw material dictated the degree of workmanship evident in the tools. The other held that the able stone worker could work even poor material. The two shelters on Hora Mountain presented a test case because the source of raw material available to the inhabitants of these two shelters had been the same. Yet the people who made the tools 10,000 years or more before their counterparts from Hora/5, chose a better quality of quartz and employed a more methodical approach in their stone work. The older inhabitants also had produced strikingly less waste material.

21

The 'later' occupants used quartz of a more crystalline nature that breaks unevenly, shatters and crumbles. The number of secondarily worked tools was very small. These were made from flakes whose edges were retouched after they had been removed from the core or primary piece of raw material. The scars left on cores by the flakes that were removed and the scars that can be seen on these flakes have such irregular shapes and show so many different directions from which they were struck, that the manner of stone tool making can only be described as irregular.

Is it not reasonable, therefore, to conclude that the able craftsman would be more sensitive to the raw materials he chose? He would go to greater trouble to find good raw material than his colleague who was less concerned about the standard of the finished product. The less discerning stone tool person who was not going to spend much time on an involved technique, would also take less trouble looking for material that was scarce. We felt that this comparison indicated that motivation would have been the critical factor. The earlier people were more motivated to produce good stone tools. Perhaps the dawn of the Iron Age and the notion of metal as a raw material were reflected in the sloppy work done during this stage of the Later Stone Age in Malawi? Someone had told someone that somewhere people were producing a material called IRON and one could use it more efficiently than stone for cutting, chopping, digging, scraping.

The analysis of stone tool assemblages has caused many people hours, days and years of hard work, gazing at the implements, cleaning them, feeling (!) them, drawing them and measuring them. With new tools and methods such as computers and statistics there was scope for many more hours, days and years of similar work consisting of weighing, measuring, comparing and analysing. Until all approaches have been proved futile or until *the* successful approach has been discovered, no self-respecting archaeologist should rest. Yet for those of us, desirous of a sense of achievement, how do we accommodate the time and effort

Diagram of irregularly worked cores and poorly worked microliths. a & b) Two cores or chunks show only two or three scars from which flakes have been removed. Small scars may reflect utilization or unsuccessful attempts of striking the stone. c & d) Two roughly shaped flakes or chips of poor quality material which breaks and shatters easily.

spent on stone tool analysis, when we feel that the result will not do very much more than verify the first impression gained by a Professor Clark or Professor Glynn Isaac after no more than a careful look at the material? The basic problem is to know the right questions. How much information can we extract from the stone artefacts we have found? How relevant is that information? Can the stone artefact tell us why it was produced - or by whom? The values and motives of the people who specialised in making stone tools changed over time for many different reasons. Can we decipher why or how? The information about their experiences is not neatly written up but has to be deciphered from archaeological remains. The student of archaeology may indulge in speculations about what happened, when and why it happened. But if these speculations are to be taken seriously, evidence has to be presented. And the evidence must be sound and stand up to the test of time. Subsequent work is bound to prove or disprove it. Students of biochemistry were making fascinating observations. But the African Eve had not yet emerged.

Other fellow students were searching for people still making and using stone tools. But these examples are rapidly disappearing as our planet is becoming more and more densely populated. Hunter-gatherer economies can no longer survive. Apart from that, it is dangerous to suppose that the values of people living by hunting and gathering have never changed.

Segments, crescents, lunates, geometrics or trapezoids

5 cm

Illustration of flakes being removed from a core

Hunter- gatherers who may still have been using stone tools until a few decades ago, have undergone as varied a history as any other people living today. Archaeologists are challenged to reconstruct these histories, at least in broad terms, as far as possible. We then hope to recognise hallmarks of human behaviour in the available evidence. Ideally this may lead us to predictions and even to ways of preventing disasters.

During my conversations with Keith Robinson I realised how rapidly the number of archaeologists working in Africa was increasing. Keith knew all the colleagues who were approximately his age personally and many of them were good friends. I knew only a few of them personally and a few more by name. In addition there were those students whom I had met in the course of my studies. But these were only a fraction of those working in Africa at this time. This changing situation demanded improved methods of communication by developing a clearly defined set of terms used in talking about the material. Keith introduced me to the differences between the crescents (microlithic stone tools) Cran Cooke meant when he talked about Khami ruins, to the ones that Desmond Clark meant when he described the Nachikufan Industries found in Zambia and the ones which he, Keith, meant when he discussed the Leopard's Kopje site in Zimbabwe. And yes, all of them might also be referred to as segments, lunates or semi—hemilemniscates, but they were all different although they were all roughly semicircular little stones with a blunted convex edge and a straight sharp edge except for the double crescents - and they were blunted on both edges. We don't know what double crescents were used for. The simple or single crescents were used as arrowheads. The blunt convex edge of the crescent was hafted onto the end of the wooden arrow and the straight, sharp edge would cut into the flesh of the prey, without then easily slipping out of the wound.

It comforted me to hear Keith Robinson express genuine pity for me in having to try and find a way through this confusing mass (or mess) of terms and stones. My decision to turn my energies to other areas of interest in the archaeological field began to harden the more I worked with the stones. I was hoping to find a site that documented a contact between a Later Stone Age hunting-and-gathering people and an Iron Age people who might have been gardeners as well as herders and whose material culture would comprise metal goods and pottery. How simple-minded I was! Life was much more complicated than this student of archaeology had imagined. The twists and turns in the lives of individuals were the ones that marked history and many individuals' histories have made up prehistory and archaeology. The short period of history reported on in written documents is marked by the accounts of individual personalities representing societies, movements and happenings. This is not the case for the huge time spans which engulf prehistory and its handmaiden, archaeology. Only in rare cases as, for instance, in the case of the Egyptian Pharaos, can individuals be identified in the archaeological record. Here in southern Africa we can only try to find evidence for developments affecting large numbers of people.

PHOPO HILL

We had studied the map of Malawi and had decided to have a good look at Lake Kazuni. This little lake near the town of Rumpi was fed by the South Rukuru River, which then continued into Lake Malawi. Again the natural beauty of the landscape was a sheer delight. The lake consisted of a pan-like depression with low ranges of hills on the periphery. At the height of the dry season there was very little water left of what was hardly more than a widening of the river's course. The meadow on which sheep or cattle could graze when we were there, probably would have been covered by water after the rains.

A bridge demarcated the point where the river entered the lake area. The banks were steep and high. They presented a textbook example of a profile of the ground, which had been accumulating in layers over long periods of time. This then was the point where we started looking for evidence of early Iron Age occupation sites. Drought is of benefit to archaeological reconnaissance work. Artefacts can be found much more easily when the ground is stripped of vegetation. Since the river had been reduced to a narrow little stream in the centre of its bed, we could examine a surface where the water might have dropped material it was carrying. We were wandering down the dry part of the riverbed with the bank of the river towering above us. A few large worked stones were among the first finds

Profile of the South Rukuru River bank close to the bridge demarcating the point where the river enters Lake Kazuni. The stick points to potsherds eroding out of the soil face.

we made. When we came to a dry gully forming a side arm, Keith decided to go and have a look on top of the bank and had soon made another find: bits of slag - the waste products of metal smelting.

 "I think it's definitely iron slag and could be very recent, lying on the surface as it is," he called out to me from a distance. In the meantime I had also found some potsherds, but they too appeared to be of a recent date, showing decorations that I had observed on pots still being used in the villages today.

"What was I really looking for?" I asked myself. I recognised a superstitious lack of courage to consciously admit what my most cherished wish was for fear of it not coming true. Picking up the next potsherd was mind-boggling.

"No," I told myself, "don't believe it, look for another one."

Out of breath although I was walking only a little faster but with my head much closer to the ground than before, I continued in the direction of the watercourse. There was another one!

"Keith!" I called at the top of my voice, "Keith, come and look!"

 As usual he was next to me within a split second - or that is how it felt.

"That's channelling," he said, referring to the smooth groove that marked the decoration associated with an early pottery tradition in East Africa.

I kept quiet, afraid of showing enthusiasm that might turn out to be unwarranted. Channelling was the distinctive feature of Kalambo ware, or channelled pottery as it was also called. Desmond Clark had found it in dateable context at his famous site, Kalambo Falls,

and it was considered the earliest Iron Age pottery in Africa south of the Sahara.
But I did not yet have much experience with pottery and was dying for Keith to say that it did, in fact, look like *real* channel ware or Kalambo pottery. He had followed another small side arm of the river and was off inspecting the section along the bank of the little tributary leading into the river. The ground was a red-brown colour and of clayey texture, well-eroded by flowing water, although it was quite dry now. I remembered that this was one of the driest spots in the whole of Malawi, according to one of the few books on Malawi available at the time.

"This is one of the richest sites I have ever seen," Keith said.
I think, he too, was perhaps reluctant to admit success quite yet, in case we just might be mistaken after all.

Keith showed me the remains of a metal furnace he had found. Apart from slag, the telltale signs of metal working on archaeological sites were remains of tuyères. These are clay pipes, which were used as mouthpieces leading the air from the bellows into the furnace. Commonly they were made by baking wet clay around a branch and firing it. The wood burnt away and the clay hardened, leaving the desired cylindrical tuyère, which would become more durable with usage as it lay in the fire and accumulated molten metal and slag.

The tuyères here at Phopo, Keith thought, were very much larger than other tuyères he had seen in South Africa and Zimbabwe. There were hundreds of fragments lying about here. A mound about two metres in diameter and approximately 50 centimetres high in the centre indicated the furnace. Keith explained how he thought that this particular one probably consisted of a circular clay wall, perhaps half or even a metre high with a number of holes near the base for the tuyères. Accordingly a number of bellows would have been positioned around the outside of the furnace. At each one of these bellows a person would have been sitting hour after hour ensuring that the fire had an adequate supply of oxygen. Inside the furnace the ore and the fuel would have been packed in alternate layers.

"Are there many variations on this method of metal smelting?" I asked.
"Some. But the point is that they all use clay and we therefore associate the knowledge of metal working with that of pottery and think that the same people who introduced pottery into southern Africa also introduced metal working."
"And the earliest pottery is the channel ware?"
"Apparently. Channel ware or dimple-based pottery. It was also called dimple-based because some of the pots have hollows or concavities in their floor. But there are some things that don' t quite fit into the picture, such as the Gokomere ware and the so-called Hottentot pottery."
"You mean the pottery they found at Mapungubwe?"
"Yes. That looks completely different. I would also love to see the pottery you have in Namibia. I don't think that looks much like the so-called Bantu pottery."
"But then most of Namibia was originally not inhabited by Bantu-speakers but by hunter-gatherer groups such as Khoe, Damara and San."
"I know. However, aren't people of the opinion that they traded their pottery from the Bantu such as the Herero and Ovambo?"
I still had a lot to learn and felt ashamed of not knowing more about what had been written about Namibia. Not that there was all that much literature, but I should have been able to recite by heart what little there was.

"Keith, do you think this might be one of the earliest Iron Age sites," and, I added "in this area?" lest it should sound too ambitious.

"Well, some of these potsherds at any rate resemble the ones from Mwavorambo that I found last year and they had a date of ±1,000 AD."

In the evening we looked over our finds. There were many sherds with very distinctive curvilinear patterns of fat, smooth grooves. Growing more confident of our identifications we got out our textbooks and compared our sherds with the illustrations. Our task now was to find a place where an excavation would reveal the material in the context of its geological layer. Thus far we had only picked up material from the surface that could have been washed there from far away by the river. The freshness of the breaks on many pieces and their position on the sides of the gully seemed to indicate that they were eroding out at this particular place but this too would have to be verified.

"We'll sink a number of test pits and depending on what we find, we can see what to do next."

"What to do and *when* to do it?" I threw in.

"I know what you mean. One always underestimates the time factor."

A terrible fear suddenly clutched me.

"Four weeks are gone already, and we haven't even found a single site that has Iron Age and Later Stone Age material in clear, neat stratification."

"How many of those did Desmond want you to find?"

"Half a dozen or so, he said in his letter."

"He doesn't want much, does he?"

"But Keith, this is to be the fieldwork for my doctoral degree. If I don't find them, I won't get it."

"Well, then I think you should start getting used to the idea of not getting it, because it is humanly impossible to discover, test and excavate half a dozen sites within a single field season. By rights these three processes should be spread over three years. The first year you just drive around looking for surface indications. The following trip you dig test pits and only when you have analysed and dated the material from your test trenches do you go out to undertake extensive excavations at the most promising sites."

"But you don't know what Desmond is like. I must do what he says."

"My dear girl, that is impossible unless you have a time machine. This I say because I do know what he is like. He has no concept of time. He expects to do things as fast as he can think them."

"Yes, but look at all he has done and is doing."

"True. And one of the reasons is Betty who is his anchor to reality. Without her he would long ago have died on some expedition into the desert on which he would have neglected to take along food and water."

The anxiety I had felt earlier on during the conversation when I was considering going out and starting the excavation by gaslight, had been soothed a little. Yet I felt that we had not yet found a single site of the sort I was after. As though he were reading my thoughts, Keith said:

"The one thing you will have to learn is that field work and discoveries cannot be dictated. The only way in which you can hope to make a contribution is by painstakingly recording whatever you find. By and by it will start fitting together and you will see a story emerging."

"Surely you must start off with a theoretical framework, and certain well-defined questions in mind."

"Theoretical framework! " He grunted. "You university people make me sick with all your theories and highfaluting language. Spend some more time on doing common sense groundwork and the theories will take care of themselves. To think that here you sit and worry about finding the *right* site when we have discovered what we have today. Honestly, Beatrice, that is not very intelligent. If I were a professor a student might just fail because she did not recognise the importance of her find."

"What chance do I have? Desmond will fail me on what I don't find and you'll fail me on what I do find?"

With a sigh I picked up one of the sherds again and looked at it. It *was* pretty wonderful to have found this site within a few hours of starting to look for it. How often does that happen, that one picks a point on the map, drives up to it, gets out and finds what one is looking for? But the little voice of insecurity and doubt was there again. What if we did not find Later Stone Age material below it?

For my first, and as it turned out, only test square, I picked an area on top of the riverbank, a few hundred yards away from its edge. I was hoping to hit the layer with the potsherds that were eroding out on the steep face of the riverbank. We cleared the vegetation, tied string to the four corner pegs of the one metre test square and started scraping away the firm dry soil in horizontal layers. Again it had been easy to hire local help. The sieve was set up so that the slight wind would not blow the dust onto us and in my note book a fresh page was entitled "Phopo Hill - surface." It was my luck to work at the base of a hill that would remind any German speaker of buttocks or 'Popo'. Thanks to the saving 'h' I decided to pronounce it with an initial 'f' sound and would claim that to be the only and correct pronunciation. I grinned at the thought of all the jokes that I would fall victim to amongst my German friends. As it turned out they were not interested!

While working in the field and thinking about the esoteric nature of my work, that is the field of archaeology, I realised that it contributed towards a gradually widening social distance between myself and the circle of people I had been in contact with during my childhood and during my short career as a grade school teacher. The concept of archaeology as a profession that could earn you a living, was foreign to the circle of friends I had. The idea of archaeology having to do with any other country than Greece and Egypt seemed illegitimate. During the sixties, due to the prevailing political climate in South Africa, and, by implication, also in Namibia or South West Africa, studying in the USA was suspect. This was well illustrated by the lengths to which I had to go in persuading people that a degree from the University of California in Berkeley was equivalent to a degree from the University of Stellenbosch in the Republic of South Africa! My lack of enthusiasm for the Apartheid regime fitted my image of an extraordinarily misled compatriot.

The top layer entitled 'Surface' at Phopo did not provide for any exciting remarks in my field notes and soon I was onto the next layer, 'Surface - 5 centimetres' below surface. The deposit was hard but could be scraped with the side of the trowel, which did not hit any obstructions. Sieving was merely a formality. The fine clayey sand merely slipped through the meshes of the sieve and nothing remained behind. Then the trowel hit something hard. A pebble. One tiny paper bag with a pebble - sole find in the spit 'Surface - 5 centimetres'. Tea-time at last.

"Strange that you aren't finding anything."

"Yes. But I'll go on for a while."

"Oh yes, you must,"

THE TIME LINE
An artist's impression

A.D. 2004

1920 Dikundu - iron smelting/Kavango
1746 D.E.I.C. coins found at Meob
1689 Drierivier cairn II/Rehoboth
1669 Drierivier cairn I/Rehoboth
1650 Copper smelting site/Rehoboth
      & Vungu Vungu/Kavango
1620 Tree cairn site/Rehoboth
1235 Gorob Plain cairn/Kuiseb
850 Kapako/Kavango
740 Gorob River Mouth cairn/Kuiseb
400 Mirabib Hill dung floor
295 Phopo Hill/Malawi
230 !Narob cairn/Kuiseb

**IRON AGE
2000 years**

B.C. / A.D.

A.D. / B.C.
400-1400 Fingira/Malawi

**LATER STONE AGE
up to 30 000 yrs ago**

3240 Mirabib Hill vegetation rich layer
3740 Charè sandy layer
4550 Mirabib Hill sandy layer
4840 Charè/much organic material
6250 Mirabib Hill - dark grey layer

8000 Otjiseva?

14730 Hora/7 Malawi

23000 Homeb silt layers

27000 Apollo II
painted stones

African eve

**MIDDLE STONE AGE
up to 150 000 yrs ago**

Homo erectus
1,8 mill. yrs ago
Olduvai

**EARLY STONE AGE
up to 3mill. yrs ago**

3 to 4 mill. yrs ago
Australopithecus

13 mill. yrs ago
Otavipithecus

30 mill. yrs ago
Arrisdrift

33

CHAPTER 3

COMING HOME TO SOUTH WEST AFRICA / NAMIBIA

I was eager to get back to Wade, to Windhoek, to another phase in my life in SWA/
Namibia. It was a shock to hear that Dr Steyn was no longer Director at the State Museum
in Windhoek. He had been promoted to the Transvaal Museum and his successor was a
man I managed to antagonise from the word *go*.

My problems at the State Museum began with the struggle to be re-appointed to the
position from which I had been given study leave under Dr Steyn. The civil servants in the
Education Department, also responsible for running the museum, wanted to re-instate me
as a Primary School teacher in a rural village rather than as an archaeologist at the Museum. Their argument was that the need for teachers was greater than the need for archaeologists.

The upper echelon of the civil service in South West Africa consisted almost exclusively of
white male Afrikaners who belonged to the clandestine Broederbond. This powerbroking
organization was committed to sustaining racist white supremacy in South Africa. The
doctrine of Christian National Education ruled supreme at the Afrikaans medium universities where the future leaders were to be educated. Balthasar Vorster had indeed succeeded Hendrik Verwoerd as President of South Africa, as Keith had speculated when we
were working on the Nyika Plateau. Also, in 1966, South Africa had lost the case against
Ethiopia and Liberia in the International Court of Justice in Den Haag. Now the political
hegemony over South West Africa was intensified. An enlightened professional female
who was graduating from the University of California in Berkeley – in the news on account
of the students' Free Speech Movement, Hippies and Flower Power – was anathema.
The private secretary to the Administrator of Sout West Africa - possibly the most influen-
tial person in the government of the time - initiated a discussion I had with him by posing
the question:
"Of what practical use is all this scientific research you people talk about?"
I pointed to the fluorescent bulb over his desk and asked:
" Does that light serve any purpose in your opinion?" He frowned and I went on:
"Products like that ultimately are the outcome of scientific research."
My undiplomatic provocation was answered in a way I might have anticipated:
"You just make me angry with stupid arguments that have nothing to do with real life."
Luckily the Administrator of South West Africa was a more liberal man and probably re-

sponsible for my appointment as archaeologist to the Windhoek State Museum. Wade and I had met him at the Administrator's Xmas party given in Swakopmund every year. The Director of the private Swakopmund Museum, Dr. Alfons Weber, had introduced us to him. As one of the four professional officers on the staff of the State Museum, I was so enthusiastic that I started working two months ahead of the official commencement of my contract. My first self-assigned task was a survey of work done by archaeologists in Namibia to date and a study of the museum collections, followed by drawing up a scheme of work to be embarked upon. The setting and much of the material was very familiar, although four years had passed since I had worked there with Rona MacCalman, who had succeeded the first qualified archaeologist to be appointed by the Government. She had left and I observed a remarkable change in myself. I was amazed at the different light in which I saw the archaeological collections, a light coloured by the knowledge and the experience I had gained in the course of graduate study and the time spent in Malawi.

STONE TUYÈRES

The point was particularly well illustrated as I studied the artefacts. I came upon a stone with a hole bored through it, which I remembered from before. A farmer from the south of the country near Bethanie had brought it in one morning and told us where he had found it on his farm. It was a heavy, dark magmatic rock, very well worked into a triangular shape with a conical hole bored straight down its central axis.

I had not thought about this stone once in all these years and it took me a few minutes to reconstruct the occasion of its arrival in the museum. A certain realization dawned on me as I inspected it more closely. There was some metal residue adhering to the small hole at the point of this triangular rock, which looked almost like a funnel. Could this be slag?! I called Wade in and he too, was intrigued by this possibility. During the few weeks he had spent with Keith and me in Malawi he had become acquainted with the current theories dealing with the introduction of metal work into southern Africa.

Not long thereafter I had a call from Ric Haig, a geologist working for a mining company. He had discovered traces of prehistoric metal working at the Onganya mine where he was employed. Over the telephone he described what once more sounded like a stone tuyère. The stone was at the mine and we arranged to go there the following weekend. It was a pleasant trip from Windhoek and I enjoyed being back in this country with which I had links much stronger than I had been aware of.

Ric had found the stone on the bank of a river that was cutting its course into the Damara system. This geologically ancient suite of rocks surfaces in the central parts of Namibia. It contains different kinds of stone such as the black mica schist and white quartz. Cobbles of this material were covering the surface. Soon we had found traces of slag. They were scattered over a very wide area.

Many of the quartz pebbles and cobbles were chipped or had flakes taken off them. Chunks that fitted into one's hand like a hammering tool had pecking marks on their surface while larger rocks had pecking marks on flat parts of their surface. Such heavy-duty tools could have been used to crush the ore. I was looking for potsherds but could not find any. Nor was there any sign of a clay furnace, let alone clay tuyères. At the mine camp Ric showed me the stone, which he had described over the telephone. I was stunned.

Traces of slag were scattered over a wide area. Quartz pebbles and cobbles showed signs of working.

There was a lump of mica schist rock a foot and a half long and almost as broad, with the top and the bottom slightly flattened, giving it the appearance of an extraordinarily large loaf of bread. A wide cylindrical hole had been bored through its centre and a thick layer of iron slag encrusted one end like the cuff of a sleeve. The stone had a pleasing soft shiny texture due to the high content of talc or soapstone in the mica schist from which it was made.

There could be no question that this was a tuyère. But a stone tuyère?! I wished Keith had been there and in my mind I went over our conversations on tuyères and Iron Age furnaces. I could not recall ever having discussed stone. When we were talking I certainly had never thought of that bored stone I had recently rediscovered in the museum collections. Tuyères made of stone. What did that imply? What did it mean?

"Maybe they didn't know about clay," Ric suggested.

"But we do find clay pots and potsherds in Namibia," Wade pointed out.

"By the way, do you know a man called Seudo?" Ric enquired.

"He asked one of our guys here the other day whether he had ever found any pots in the veld."

"That's Mr Sydow, an amateur archaeologist with the finest collection of prehistoric clay pots in the country. He has just published a useful description of pre-European pottery in Namibia."

"What are his theories - if he has any?"

"Oh, he does indeed have theories. The discussions I have had with him got bogged down when it came to theories which he felt had been adequately proven and should therefore be accepted as fact."

"You seem to be referring to a specific theory he has - tell me about it."

This led into a conversation about theories and hypotheses; about Eurocentric biases and about the universal phenomenon reflected in the saying that the prophet/ess is not respected in his/her own land. The ancestors of local people could not possibly have been skilled craftsmen or even artists!

Consequently the assumption prevailed that all rock art in Namibia must have been executed by people 'with culture' who must have come from far away because the indigenous population of Namibia was considered to be 'without culture'. Anything that appeared to have been sophisticated or beautiful was explained in terms of it having been brought in by people from elsewhere. Curiously the same principle was used in dealing with evil matters. Communism, liberalism and any ideas opposing Apartheid were brought in from the outside as well…

Some of the pottery found in Namibia displayed a shape reminiscent of pots with pointed bases and lugs, also made in Western Europe during prehistoric times. Consequently it was suggested that the pots found in Namibia were made by visitors from Denmark. Similarly metal work had been assigned to Bantu speaking peoples of West or East Africa and any traces of prehistoric metalworking were interpreted as contact with people from those regions. Could stone tuyères represent an independent invention of metal working here in Namibia?

On the drive back to Windhoek I felt elated. This was more *fieldwork* right here where I felt at home and where I enjoyed being at home so consciously. This feeling was enhanced because I could share it so meaningfully with Wade, the fellow anthropologist. We stopped to speak to a few farm workers and I tested my limited knowledge of the local language. I tasted the benefit of being familiar with an area and its people. There was a feeling of security in knowing approximately how far apart homesteads and farmhouses were situated, in recognizing ethnic or tribal differences and in being able to greet people in their own language, even if that alone already exhausted my vocabulary. It felt good to be accepted as a local, rather than as a stranger. This was relative because, after all, I was white and we were living in the sixties in the land where Apartheid was having its heyday. I decided that as soon as my dissertation was completed I would devote myself to learning, or rather re-learning, the Damara language.

As I grew up as the only child of my parents on a farm in the Namib Desert, my playmates were Damara children and my mother recalled that I conversed fluently with them in their language. I remembered a little boy of whom I had been particularly fond. His name was Konrad and my parents thought he was a 'skelm'… But I liked his smooth high forehead on which the arteries would stand out when he laughed and showed a row of flashing white teeth. The same veins would protrude when he was close to tears and his upper lip was trembling. When we were out in the veld he made me feel safe when he guided me along a tricky path or over a narrow rock ledge on the mountainside. When I had to walk home at midday the loose sand of the riverbed I had to cross was as hot as a bed of coals to my bare feet. Konrad would take my hand and make me run across it as fast as I could.

There was a game involving two teams running and then half jumping and half rolling over old car tyres that had been set in motion. In the process one had to try to run over a member of the other team. I remember the excitement and some fear of getting hurt, the screaming and the shouting with the rolling tyres gathering momentum as they rolled downhill. Suddenly Konrad stopped the game. He said that care should be taken not to hurt me else my father would take away the tyres. I never found out whether my father had said so.

When I left the farm to go to school in Swakopmund I did not get along with the other children. I was an outsider and became the victim of a little gang of girls who ridiculed and teased me. I cried every morning that I had to go to school. Time seemed interminable and the comfort of holidays was meaningless because they were too far off. I seriously contemplated hanging myself by standing on a chair next to a window with the cord of my mother's bathrobe around my neck. I was going to tie the other end to the window frame and would then kick away the chair I was standing on. I also considered walking along the track across the desert, which we travelled when we came from the farm.

But before I could implement either of these dark plans my fortune changed, when Dorothee, a courageous little girl in my class, suddenly declared herself my friend. We got on well together and ignored the other children. It seemed only natural to invite Dorothee to come and visit me during the holidays. On our arrival at the farm a large mug was standing on the kitchen table. I recognised the yellow flower on blue enamel background. It was Konrad's mug and it was filled with the small red berries I knew only too well. They came from a wild bush and were part of the 'veldkos ' that I had often been out to collect with Konrad and his family.

The following day, when I was sitting on the veranda playing a card game with Dorothee I had the feeling of someone watching me. As I turned around I noticed someone peeping around the corner of the house. I jumped up and shouted:
"Konrad, come play with us."
But he had disappeared. I went to look for him and found him standing behind the kennels. We looked at each other and were both very embarrassed. His lips trembled and the veins stood out on his forehead. He said:
"You have other friends now," and ran away.
"Why are you crying?" Dorothee asked.
"I don't want to play cards any more," I said.

I have been trying to recall how I talked to Konrad but have forgotten any awareness of a particular language being spoken. I could only hope that on learning the language again I would recognise words or phrases and that they would stimulate my subconscious to get in touch with my conscious mind again. Such reflections came about as a result of my studies in anthropology. The grade-school which I attended in Swakopmund reflected the racist apartheid ideology, which effectively discouraged any unprejudiced interest in 'primitive' people and their lives or language.

We were lucky in having good teachers who nevertheless managed to make us think. None of them, however, dared to promote critical thinking with regard to our own society. They knew only too well that those in power would not tolerate any deviation from what was prescribed by political policy. My Jewish background and my parents, who belonged to the opposition party, contributed to my dissension. Two of our teachers were very friendly with my parents and privately critical of the system. One of them had escaped the holocaust and cleverly hid her background until she died. I owe both of them a great debt as excellent teachers.

Dr Ruth Hohenstein was our teacher in Grade 3. One day she told us about Heinrich Schliemann and how he had discovered the city of Troy that had been buried for centuries. That was when I decided to become an archaeologist. It was my parents' favourite piece of dinner conversation for a long time. When I took the matter up in High School my Dad sat me down and spoke seriously.
"You know that I love you very much and I do think Archaeology is a fascinating subject. But unfortunately it requires a great deal of money to work as an archaeologist." He told me about an archaeological expedition that had been reported on and what it involved in terms of people and equipment.
"Unfortunately, my darling ("mein Tochterchen" in the East Prussian dialect), I cannot offer you such possibilities. Therefore please think about another profession."
I took this to heart and when a team of psychologists came to offer career guidance at the Swakopmund High School, I was very keen to see them. Every one in our class took an I.Q. test and was then called in for a discussion. A man and a woman were conducting these interviews and asked me what I wanted to be.
"An Archaeologist?"
"Yes"
"Do you know what that is?"
"Yes"
" There is no place in South Africa where you can learn that. Think of something else."
"Then I would like to study Geology."
"What?! But that is not a profession for a woman."
"Then I don't know what to do."
"Don't you want to be a teacher?"
"No."
"What about a secretary?"
"No."
"Your strength lies in languages. Have you ever thought about being an interpreter?"
I wanted to know a bit more about that and was intrigued by the possibility of being an interpreter for the United Nations Organization in New York.

For many years I referred to this career guidance intervention as having caused a five-year detour in my education. I went to famous Heidelberg in Germany, to enrol at one of the two world-renowned schools for interpreters. In spite of the Student Prince and the romantic environment, I was a desperately unhappy seventeen year-old on the banks of the Neckar. I went home after a year to join my mother in running a shop in Swakopmund. I was utterly disillusioned with academe and universities and determined to promote my own educa-tion via correspondence courses with the University of South Africa. I took Archaeology and Anthropology as my main courses. The following year was not very satisfactory either and I owe it to two wonderful friends from High School days, Gernot and Armin Häussler, who took me to task and made me apply for a bursary to go to the Teachers Training College in CapeTown.

CHAPTER 4

WORK AT THE WINDHOEK STATE MUSEUM

Fieldwork was a highly respected activity at the Windhoek State Museum. The taxidermist would go on extended fieldtrips, often to areas where ordinary people could only go with special Permits. These were collecting trips. The museum officers were well-equipped with 4x4 trucks, many different kinds of guns and well-trained assistants. On returning to the museum the colleagues could admire small elephants or even rhino, antelopes and rare birds that had been collected. The workshops would be humming with activity surrounding the stuffing and mounting of the specimens that had been collected. Frequently other government officials and friends of the museum staff decorated their homes with expertly prepared items of this sort. Well-stuffed Kudu heads with horns were going for R80,00 a piece.....

Although my fieldwork did not have quite that status, it did allow me to go on my small expeditions according to the provision I had managed to make in the budget. When I was working at the Museum in Windhoek I continued with my survey of the collections, specifically looking out for more tuyères. I had checked the catalogue but only two clay tuyères had been recorded and they were from the Kavango River Region. I found several items described as stones with holes. I checked them out and discovered another three stone tuyères right there in the museum collection. They had all been found in the central and southern parts of the Namibia. It turned out that the ethnologist had another specimen in his collection, unfortunately without any data. So we didn't know who found it or where it came from. The museum's secretary, too, had seen a similar stone on her father's farm, which was situated not far from Windhoek.

Within a few weeks I had traced fourteen stone tuyères. By contrast, there were no clay tuyères and no records or indications of clay furnaces found in central or southern Namibia. Dr Hans Scholz, a soil scientist, had reassured me that the fact that clay had not been used in the process of working metal could not be ascribed to an absence of usable raw clay. There was no shortage of clay along river courses nor was there a shortage of anthills.

I had quite consciously also registered the frequent occurrence of anthills and termite mounds which had often been pointed out as a source of clay to me in Malawi. Not far

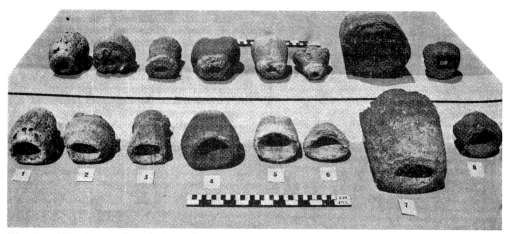

We placed the stone tuyères in front of a mirror so that both sides of these pipes could be seen on a photograph

Part of the museum exhibit displayed the stone tuyère found by Ric Haig

from Windhoek there was a quarry where clay bricks had been made. Many farmhouses were built with clay bricks and traditionally, Namibians had been aware of the qualities of clay and had used it for building and plastering their houses. Clay pots were not being made commonly any more but there were reliable reports of conversations with old Damara people who knew what clay pots were and how they were made.

My work focused on stone tuyères, their distribution and the location of sites with the aim of finding a place suitable for excavating a furnace associated with stone tuyères. To put my thoughts into slightly better order, I drew up a report on Iron Age features in Namibia. The aim was to outline a number of approaches that might be employed in investigating the question of how knowledge of potmaking and metalworking had developed in an area traditionally inhabited by hunter-gatherers. The image of hunter-gatherers did not cater for work with burnt clay or metal.

An exhibit on stone tuyères supplemented my report. The museum had a number of showcases at strategic positions in town. Members of staff had taken it upon themselves to prepare temporary exhibits for these glass cases, which would inform the public of ongoing research work at the museum and stimulate people to visit the museum. Such programmes, and visiting scientists or museum staff, who were giving bi-weekly lectures on their work at the museum contributed to making the young institution a small, but vibrant centre of activity. For this we had to thank Dr Steyn, who had not only been a scientist of international stature but who had also been an excellent administrator with vision who could stimulate his staff into concerted action. Unfortunately many of the useful habits Dr Steyn had promoted were gradually being neglected. Staff meetings, which had been wonderful opportunities to report on one's work and to hear about the work of colleagues, had deteriorated into gossip sessions and opportunities for castigating members of staff.

I gained strength from the resolution that the best way in which I could honour the people whose work I had admired so deeply was to try and continue doing work of which they would approve. I drew up a rigorous timetable of hours I was going to devote to the writing up of my doctoral thesis on the research in Malawi and to regular library work. I decided to prepare for the publication of a report on excavations in the Erongo Mountains done a number of years before by Rona MacCalman and a group of dedicated amateur archaeologists like Mr Sydow and Mr Viereck.

MEOB BAY

Time and again mining companies and people working for them proved extremely helpful and co-operative. One morning I had a call from Helge Laursen, an American geologist working for Tide Water Minerals, a mining company. They were working on a rather inaccessible part of our desert coast and Mr Laursen had found signs of human occupation. He found it incredible that people without our technology could have survived in an area as inhospitable as that along the sand dune coast of the Namib Desert and wanted to know whether we had any previous records of prehistoric dwellers along the coast.

I told him about the reports of the first European visitors to the coast during the fifteenth and sixteenth centuries and reminded him of Jan van Riebeeck's diary. Everywhere beach combers (or Strandlopers) were mentioned - people who roamed the coasts and lived on the products of the sea and the shore. In some cases they also had cattle.

"Well, I'm fascinated," he said, "and I very much want you to come and have a look at the sites around Meob Bay."

I replied that I would very much like to and visualised an expedition of two or three Land Rovers driving - or rather being pushed - across the sand dunes.

"Do you drive down along the coast from Walvis Bay," I asked, "or do you by any chance approach Meob Bay across country from Sossus Vlei?"

"Oh no! We fly in every week."

"With Suidwes Lugdiens? I didn't know they could land there."

And in my mind I was now filling out forms in centuplicate months ahead of time to go to Pretoria in application for a flying expedition to the diamond area along the coast.

That would have to be the procedure under the new regime at the museum.

"No, we have our own planes and you don't need to worry about getting there or staying there. We have a well-equipped camp. You only need to take the equipment you need for your work. I usually go on Monday or Tuesday and stay a week or so. Let me know when it will suit you to go."

"Could my husband come along?"

"But of course."

It was heartening to hear an American accent again and to have coupled with it that generosity of doing things. This way attention could be focussed on the essential things. Automatically one gave the very best to one's work. I remember how it had struck me in Malawi that eating, sleeping and dressing were matters one learned to perform within as short a time as possible, so that one could pay maximum attention to more essential things. Ultimately it is a question of values and priorities.

While it is critical that the basic necessities sustaining one's material existence be taken care of, there are the demands of the mind and the soul. People who are totally dedicated to ideas will forego the material requirements. However, I was pleased to discover that there were ways of doing both, that is of living comfortably albeit it modestly, and at the same time devoting oneself to such an exciting pastime as scientific research. Perhaps the telling difference between the two worlds I was straddling depended on whether money was available or not. As history would teach us economic freedom and stability accompanies many other phenomena such as health care, art, research and entertainment.

The difference in approach, which I sensed between the American way of doing things and the Namibian way was, I felt, illustrated by my acquisition of a drawing board. I had found one in a local shop that answered my needs of size, weight and quality very well. It was not cheap but considering that it was a basic piece of equipment in an archaeologist's toolkit and that it came with a well-made protective case, it was good value for money, I thought. When the Director of the Museum saw the price, he said:

"We'll make you one," picked up the phone and discussed the technical details of making a drawing board with the museum's carpenter. I admired the practical knowledge he had and was glad he obviously did not consider it below his dignity to get involved in some handiwork. I was slightly embarrassed the following day when I walked into the Museum workshop and found my Director on his knees gluing together strips of wood for my future drawing board. When I was asked to come and inspect it I did not know how to react to the furrows between the wooden boards where the glue was hardening into little lumps. It was decided that the whole board would be covered with thick linoleum, which would be glued down with a hot clothes' iron. The iron came off a little the worse for wear.

At the end of the day I had a solid, heavy drawing board without a protective case. But it had all been done with good intentions, I told myself, and the drawing board was ready for me to take to Meob Bay. I resolved that I would simply have to unlearn some of the efficient American habits and get used to African habits. Luckily Wade would be there to help me carry my heavy equipment!

The flight from Windhoek across the rugged Khomas Hochland and the Namib Desert with its plains bordering on the evenly spaced longitudinal ranges of sand dunes was a fascinating experience.

Often when I was in a plane I wondered how maps had ever been drawn before people had seen the surface of the earth from the air. The Khomas Hochland with its multitude of angularly protruding ribs of black mica-schist rocks looked utterly rough and inhospitable. Now and again we spotted a farmhouse or a dam and circular bare patches where sheep and cattle spent the night in enclosures or kraals. I was looking out for structures or formations that might be archaeologically significant but realised that one would have to devote more time to flying over smaller areas. There was not enough time to fix one's attention on one or other odd looking grouping of stones or patch of vegetation that the eye might pick out before it was already out of sight. Also the surface one had to search in this canyon-like area was too vast to be taken in during a direct flight.

Smooth expanses of plains with Inselberge protruding, partially covered up by dune sand

Once we had crossed the drop of the escarpment onto the plain of the Namib one's eyes could rest on the smooth expanses of plains out of which an occasional Inselberg would rise here and there. This was the landscape to which I had the closest affinity. One sweeping look took in a vast flat space with one or two mountains. The vegetation was extremely sparse and a number of different patterns could be discerned on the ground. Most of these were probably of a geological nature and yet I felt that it would be a worth-while project at some time in the future to scan the area thoroughly from a plane. Some day, I thought dreamily, there would be posts for a whole team of archaeologists and their assistants and I would be at the centre, co-ordinating and guiding. It was fun sharing these thoughts with Wade, although he always seemed a little reluctant to take them as seriously as I would have liked him to.

Evenly spaced longitudinal ranges of sand dunes

The first dunes appeared distinctly, as though they were drawn in with a sharp pencil. Isolated tufts of yellow grass studded their smooth, dark red surface. Here and there little drainage channels marked by a few thorn trees and bushes tried to penetrate this velvety surface from the east. Masses of sand arranged in long chains of sand mountains were running almost directly north - south. What a barren, what a desolate area! One could not help imagining what it must be like on the ground. The accounts of expeditions that had lost their way and had only barely survived came to mind. I also thought of fortune seekers going secretly into the diamond area never to be heard of again because they had per-ished miserably of thirst and exposure. There was an imperceptible change in the colour of the sand as we approached the coast. The deep orange-red of the sand on the eastern edge of the dune-field was turning into a light-yellow or grey colour.
"Would you like us to fly over the area before we land?" Helge asked.
"Please. That would be terrific."

The dunes meet the sea at the southern point of Meob Bay

He pointed out where the dunes met the sea:
"The mud flats that stretch around Conception Bay start a few miles further north of that point. Quite a bit of the coastal stretch between Meob and Conception is artificially bare of sand because it was literally swept away by the German diamond diggers at the beginning of the century."
"What are those dark specks there in the distance?" I asked.
"Gee, you've got good eyesight. I think those must be the remnants of some of their old mining shacks. You know we are also going to stay in the old wooden houses put up by that same mining group at Meob during German times."
"Aren't they all covered by dune sand?"
"No. You see just as at Conception and also at Sandwich Harbour, north of there as well as at Walvis Bay we have a lagoon forming behind a sandspit. As time passes the lagoon silts up and one gets mud flats and salt pans and apparently it takes the dunes quite a while to cover such areas."
"But they cover it eventually?" Wade asked.
"Well, it would seem so. And they always move in from the south since that is the direction of the prevailing wind."
We had turned around and were flying south again, crossing a barren depression between the ocean on the one side and the dunes on the other. In a straight line across the widest part there was some vegetation covering low hummocks of sand. Amongst these, not far from the edge of the saltpan I saw the wooden shacks Helge had mentioned. They were neatly arranged around an L-shaped yard with little catwalks leading from door to door across the sand.
"There must be fresh water here for this vegetation to exist," I remarked.
"Yes, there is. You see, I think this is a silted up river estuary. In this triangular area, which is wedged in between the ocean and the dunes one can find fresh water within one or two metres from the surface. One of the waterholes used by the Germans is right at the southern apex of this triangle"

"Is that Fishersbrunn? Or in English that would be - Fisherman's Fountain?" I asked.
"Correct. And Reutersbrunn - the fountain of Mr Reuter... you see over there right behind the camp."
"So our prehistoric inhabitants would not have been wanting for lack of water," Wade remarked.
"No, not once they were here. But how did they get here?" Helge wanted to know.
Good question, I thought. The next place with fresh water south of here was miles away at Spencer Bay. Conception Bay to the north was not all that far. But inland? Imagine crossing those high dune ridges on foot.
"The Uri-Hauchab Mountains which are like an oasis in this sand sea are about 150 kilometres south-east of here," said Helge as though reading my thoughts.
"Where did you find the artefacts you mentioned on the phone," I wanted to know.
"There are several concentrations scattered all over this vegetated area."

We were going down to land, the saltpan providing a marvellous airstrip. The people in the camp had spotted us long before and a Land Rover was there to fetch us. The air was fresh and salty and a mist bank was coming in from the ocean. Wade and I were shown to a room of our own with a large carpet on the floor and beds all made up but for our sleeping bags. For a moment I felt as though I had arrived at some beach side hotel for a holiday. But how many people, whether on holiday or not, were privileged to have an experience like this? Once more the realization of how fortunate I was washed over me like a wave imbuing me with a keen feeling of strength and enthusiasm.

I tied a scarf over my hair and got into the little Willys Jeep in which Helge was to take us to the closest archaeological site before darkness fell. The surface of the ground was dark grey and damp with white patches where salt concentrations showed up. Shells showed up in a similarly white colour. We pulled up next to a mound covered with white clamshells. A closer look revealed a host of other objects scattered among them. There were potsherds and chips of stone; scraps of metal and fragments of ostrich egg shell; pieces of bone and wood.
"This is quite fantastic!" I exclaimed, "and I wish I could hold you up as a shining example to all other potential lay archaeologists."
"Why do you say that?"
"Because you took me to the site instead of trying to bring the site to me."
"I see what you mean. Perhaps that is because of the geological background I have. One must see things in their context, otherwise they just don't make sense."
"You are so right. The trouble is that so very few people realise this."
"Mind you, I must tell you that I did feel tempted to pick up some of those very interesting large sherds with handles on them because I was afraid that if for some reason I would not be able to bring you here, they would just be destroyed by a gemsbok walking over them or something like that."
"A gemsbok?!" I asked incredulously.
"Yes, didn't you know there were gemsbok here?"
Certainly not. The picture was getting more and more interesting. Well, yes that was of course a problem to bear in mind. If an artefact is threatened by immediate destruction it is advisable to try and save it. Unfortunately the existence of many artefacts is so much more endangered once they get into the possession of private individuals than if they are just left exposed to natural hazards.
"Isn't it strange how things lose their fascination once they are in our pockets or in our garages? They so easily change from desirable, exotic objects to cumbersome baggage,"

Helge Laursen remarked.

"Isn't that ever true? I have often wondered whether that is a very significant difference in the mentality of our techno-society and the hunter-gatherer society: the attitude towards possessions. We are geared towards acquiring goods individually and take responsibility for them singly; consequently one tends to loose interest in an item once it belongs to someone else. It's his/hers or theirs and does not have anything to do with us any longer, almost as though the prime purpose of everything is to be possessed. And once it is ours, we can lose or destroy it because we *own* it. By contrast many people with a poor material culture have a different ethic. Here it is dangerous to possess more than the next person because it might incur his envy and that is a sentiment that should be avoided at all cost when you live in a small group of interdependent people." Wade, the Anthropologist, had come into his own.

A depression with vegetation covering low hummocks of sand

"What do they do with their possessions?" Helge was curious.

"They always make sure they don't keep anything that someone else wants very badly for too long. Then they hand it on." Wade explained.

"Does that also apply to wives?"

"No, only to husbands." I couldn't resist interjecting.

The next morning there was thick fog and I was glad of my heavy clothing. Again we set off in the little jeep to do a proper survey. This task was greatly facilitated by a grid the mine had put over the whole area. I could refer to numbered pegs, which in turn were related to a map. We were driving very slowly and I turned around to look at our tracks. A jackal was following in them! When we stopped the jackal stopped too and sniffed the air. "You know, when I looked at the map after you first called me, I visualised a habitat entirely dominated by the ocean. I can't get over all the animal and plant life on the land."

"You should talk to Digby. He's a kind of nut, but he talks about living off the land here."

"That would be an interesting experiment, although I suppose one should expand the concept slightly and make it 'land and sea'." Helge chuckled, and said:

"Yes I think he might be a little put out if you tried to take his fishing line away from him. By the way, is there any record of prehistoric fishing?"

"Actually the history of living along the edge of water, be it fresh or sea, is much more involved and interesting than the literature has so far given it credit for. There is a host of data on fish hooks, possible weights for nets, fish traps built of stone on shallow rocky coasts and piles of sea-food refuse in shelters and on open occupation sites all around our coast. "

"How far back do the dates for these sites go?"

"This is one of the most interesting points about the whole thing. I think fishing might be at least as old as hunting. Isn't it remarkable that the very earliest tools are found along river courses? The Klasies River Mouth shelter on the south coast of South Africa contains an accurately dated deposit going back 30,000 years."

Helge whistled through his teeth.

"Do you find tools as old as that in Namibia?"

"As old as 30,000? Oh yes, and much older."

"Really? Where and how are they dated, because the range of carbon 14 dating is limited to approximately 50,000 only, isn't it?"

"That's right,"

How different it was talking to a geologist who was used to working with time periods millions of years long. To him a mere 57,000 years was very recent history.

"The older the sites are the more difficult it is to get direct dates, that is, to find dateable material in direct association with them. Therefore many dates are based on comparisons with implements that have been found in dated contexts, such as at Kalambo Falls in Zambia, or at Olduvai Gorge or at the South African sites such as the Cave of Hearths in the Transvaal."

"What period of time does your Early Stone Age cover?"

"Helge, you do insist on talking about age."

"Would you rather I talked about dating?"

"Well.... yes... the older things get, the more difficult they are to date —"

"I agree," he threw in.

"And archaeologists and geologists are known to have played dangerous dating games by engaging in circular arguments. An alluvial terrace near Windhoek was dated in the following way: a geologist found a Middle Stone Age point in it and concluded that the terrace dated back to Middle Stone Age times which were estimated to have started over a hundred and fifty thousand years ago. Subsequently another archaeological find was made and dated according to the age suggested by the geologist. The point is simply that one has to be very cautious about assigning a particular age to an artefact that cannot be dated directly. Before the radio carbon method of dating was developed the whole system of dating Stone Age material was one of guesstimation more than anything else. The most reliable dating was known as relative dating in contrast to absolute direct dating. In other words, only if you found things in a layer above other things could you assume that the upper layer was younger than the one beneath it. And even there, terrible mistakes could be made."

"Such as?"

"Sometimes refuse pits are dug into the floor of a site which covered an older site. The content of such a hole may then be found below the previous living surface thereby upsetting the logical sequence of younger material lying on top of older stuff."

"Similar things can happen with geological deposits," Helge commented,

"Just think of the scramble one can find in breccia when all sorts of materials are baked together in some or other matrix."

I could only agree and went on:

"But to get back to your original question about the Early Stone Age. Before radiometric dating techniques were developed, a great deal of dating was based on estimation. It turned out that these estimates were almost consistently too conservative. In other words, the radiometric dating techniques showed things to be much older than had been thought and with every new discovery ages get pushed further and further back. When I started my studies I was led to consider the Early Stone Age as having lasted from the beginnings of tool making until roughly fifty thousand years ago. The earliest date that I remember was 1,8 million years obtained for Early Stone Age tools at Olduvai. Handaxes and cleavers were the index tools for this time period. A gradual change in tools then came about which led to the manufacture of smaller implements shaped like points and blades, which were assigned to the Middle Stone Age. This was thought to have lasted until approximately 5-10,000 years ago before the Later Stone Age would evolve with even smaller tools. The Iron Age covering roughly the past 2000 years has only been recognised fairly recently."

"And what is the picture today?"

" Well, the Later Stone Age has in some places been shown to go back as far as 20,000 or even 30,000years. Many people would today consider the Middle Stone Age as having commenced as early as 150,000 years ago. The beginnings of tool making and thus the Early Stone Age are now placed as far back as 2.5million years if not even more."

While I was pronouncing these dates I was wondering whether my colleagues elsewhere in the world would agree!

"So then, what do you think about our finds here?"

"Well, let's see: The metal scraps and coins that we find must post-date boats along this coast, which probably means post 1500 AD. That means we are ruling out the early Greeks and the reports by Herodotus of visits to the African coasts. The stone artefacts are so rough and undifferentiated that one can hardly say anything about them at all. Such irregularly shaped chips and flakes could have been produced at any point of the human calendar. They could represent the very first attempts of stone tool making or they could indicate a degeneration of the technique of stone tool making. In this case I would assume the latter instance to be the case. There are ethnographic reports of Himba in the Kaokoveld still today making and - or using stone artefacts. But the examples that I have seen are very rough and ready."

"Say, the Kaokoveld should also be an interesting area for you. Have you ever been there?"

"No, unfortunately not," Wade responded.

"But we have often talked about it. A year or two of ethno-archaeology in Kaokoland would be like the jackpot for Beatrice."

"Wouldn't you find that a bit lonely?"

"There are people living there - the ones we want to know more about. But I do agree that it would be easier if there were one or two other persons with whom you could talk about the things you were doing in your own language - literally and figuratively. The great problem would be the language. One has to know a language very well, particularly if one wants to overcome major cultural differences that do exist, after all," I replied.

"Then you don't agree completely with our American attitude of total equality?" Helge wanted to know.

" I honestly learned the real meaning of the word equality only in the U.S. But simultaneously I also learned the wisdom in the phrase 'equal is not the same'. Although that message is simple, I'm afraid I went for many years without properly comprehending it."

"You mean giving someone the same opportunity or accepting him on the same conditions as you would any other person does not mean that in fact he is like all others?"

51

Helge was really interested in this issue.

"Precisely. Although you may approach all people objectively, you will form your own opinion, which will be influenced by the values you have, whether you are aware of it or not. When it comes to living with people at close quarters it is very reassuring if they share those little habits that constitute so much of our daily routine. Looked at in isolation and in the light of cold logic, they may be very insignificant but over a longer time period it can be very disconcerting to be continually confronted with unexpected and unfamiliar actions or reactions, no matter how unimportant they may be in themselves," I added.

"Do you think that is what people call culture shock?"

"I think that may be part of it. Don't the psychologists say that when you consistently present someone with unexpected situations he loses his or her self-confidence and eventually starts feeling utterly insecure?" Wade asked rhetorically.

"Yes, and the final step is distrusting yourself. That is a technique employed by some of the totalitarian police states when they interrogate political prisoners. They try and make the person believe that he is suffering from loss of memory."

I shuddered. The sun was coming out and the ocean lay beyond a white strip of beach like a dark blue pond. I could not help wondering whether it would get warm enough to go for a swim. Would people living in a surrounding like this also think up ways of mental torture? What motivated people or influenced the behaviour of our species? Nature versus nurture? An age-old argument. Did our genetic make-up determine how we behaved or what we achieved or was the environment, training and education responsible for people's behaviour?

Wade and I were now starting to lay out the first test pit on top of a small shell midden quite close to the shore. Helge had left because he had to do work of his own but promised to send one or two of his young field assistants to help us with the digging. We took the opportunity of being alone and took a dip in the sea. It was exhilarating and I indulged in the awareness of probably being the only woman on a few hundred kilometres of desert coast, who was at this moment enjoying a swim. With my tan I did not quite make it as a white woman, I thought, and wondered whether some ancient honey-skinned queen of this region might perhaps be looking at us from the dim and distant past, wondering what the hell we were doing, scratching around in her rubbish heap.

I was associating her with a group of ancestral San or Khoe.

'Well, Baby,' I thought, 'I'm sure you had oddballs in your group. Why, do you think, should we be so different?'

'Well, Baby,' I heard her reply in an unfamiliar accent, 'perhaps we were fewer, but I assure you, our range and degree of oddballness did not come anywhere close to yours.'

'True' I said, 'we call it specialization'.

A misty look came into her eyes and she slowly turned her sovereign head away looking in some other direction or time dimension.

Perhaps the future... I drew in my breath, rolling my eyes as I tried to get back to reality.

It was impossible to keep the walls of the test square vertical for a depth of more than about twenty centimetres before it would start caving in under the loose sand. The layer of shells covering these mounds or middens was also about twenty centimetres deep. They were tightly packed with some ash and burnt ground sandwiched in amongst them. It was doubtful whether one could get a useful carbon 14 date from this material. There was not much charcoal at all and none of it very deep below the surface. I was under the impression that the dating of shells was tricky because they could have accumulated secondary carbon from the water in which they were living rather than directly out of the atmosphere and a count of that carbon then would not tell one the age of the shell but rather that of the water.

We collected samples of the shells and regretted not knowing more about the ancient habits of eating shellfish. The shell of a large oyster was particularly puzzling. It was massive and was at least semi-fossilised and I had never seen anything resembling it on the part of the coast with which I was familiar. Nor could I identify any of the bones we were finding with any certainty, beyond the fact that many of them were fish bones.

Surface of a midden with bone, stone, shell, pottery and fire residue (1:8)

As we were moving on to test another midden I had marked on account of the variety of items scattered over its surface we were again talking about how ideal a place this would be for a concerted interdisciplinary team effort. Elizabeth Voigt of the Transvaal Museum and an anthropologist from East London had done some work on the shellfish eating habits of natives along the east coast of southern Africa. Admittedly, the shells from the west coast probably were a different kettle of fish so to speak, but perhaps Fritz Schülein, a marine biologist working for the Institute of Fisheries Research in Walvis Bay, could help with that. One would also require a geologist or geomorphologist to explain these odd bays, ancient river estuaries or promontories. We imagined organising a research expedition with all these specialists and student assistants. Over weekends, we fantasised, teams of enthusiastic student helpers could undertake walking expeditions in different directions to see how far they could get on the resources of the area - guided by Digby….He belonged to a rare group of individualists one met from time to time in southern Africa. They often lived a dream far from the gregarious society, which had the habit of prescribing manners or certain kinds of behaviour. Digby was infatuated with living in remote Meob Bay where time seemed to resemble a huge playing field. There he could move to be a few centuries away from the here and now. There were no strings tying him down or preventing him from living the way he chose. We others were incidental and he easily accommodated us in his world. That was the impression he made on me in the course of these few days at Meob.

In the evening we had a sample of what the land and the sea here had to offer in the line of food. One of Helge's assistants, who was of French extraction, was an excellent cook and Digby, the local hunter-gatherer, supplied him with the ingredients for a superb bouillabaisse. The soft white clams were delicious. They were simply put in a pot onto the fire and secreted a tasty, juicy sauce. I was afraid I would burst when that course was followed by yet another one, consisting of delectable crayfish tails. There was an inordinate pile of them and I was assured that some of them, at any rate, could be kept in the fridge. The hours and many of the crayfish tails were, however, quickly consumed in the pleasant atmosphere around the fire place which resourceful miners had built into the wall of a semi-enclosed veranda. The open space between the roof and the waist-high wall served a very useful purpose for getting rid of food waste such as bones and bread crusts.
"Doesn't that attract a lot of vermin?" I asked
"Oh no", one of the chaps said, and shone his torch out into the yard.
"Look!"
There in the beam of his torch were two jackals, eating away at the leftovers of our meal. A little later I went to fetch something from my room and nearly died of fright when a creature jumped up from my sleeping bag. Another jackal! I closed the window and locked the door before I went back to the 'dining room'.
Driving to the sites with Digby in the Willy's Jeep was great fun. One could either race along the beach dodging the waves as one went, or take up the challenge of crossing the dunes. This required special skill and knowledge of where the sand was tightly packed on the windward side thus presenting a surface on which it was safe to drive; or where the sand was so loose that one could only get the vehicle to slide down the sand at a steep angle. I never tired of the spectacle presented by the swift, smooth lines of the dunes and the pure soft sand. My eyes were gliding along the gently rising slope of a shallow dune close to the shore when they hit on some foreign objects.

A curious little pavement of cobbles in a sea of sand, before "excavation"

I pointed them out and then Digby said:

"Yes, that is what I was looking for. I wanted to show them to you. I think it's strange to find these isolated cobbles here in all this sand."

There was a row of large, water-worn cobbles of quartz and a black fine-grained rock, protruding from the surface of smooth dune sand.

"I think there are some more stones lower down, because on some days the wind blows the sand away and one can see them," Digby commented.

"What do you think it is?" I asked.

"Gee, I don't know. We think it's where someone may have hidden a bag of diamonds," he joked.

"Why haven't you had a look yet?"

"We thought that was the work of the archaeologist."

"I see. Well, if they are worked into tools, that would of course be the case," I said, thinking how even a tiny diamond hand-axe would take care of our financial problems for the rest of our lives.

"What are you going to do?" Wade asked.

"I wish I knew! Let's first go and finish the square we started and that will give me time to think about it and decide."

We were finding a number of interesting things in the test square that we had put down on top of the midden. There were a number of copper coins imprinted with the sign of the Dutch East India Company. On one of them one could decipher the date 1746, a good indication of an absolute date. There were copper beads but no glass beads, which might have been dated according to their appearance and consistency. Strips of metal were twisted into odd shapes. One reminded me of the cigar-shaped pipes used by workers on our farm. The neck of a dark-green glass bottle was evenly cut off from the rest of the bottle, which we could not find. I was wondering whether that bottleneck too, might have served as a pipe or whether the aim of the exercise had been the other half, which would have made a handsome glass or mug.

A piece of horn or tusk was evenly shaped into a pointed, needle shaped object, which out of context, I would have said, was a hatpin. In this association, it undoubtedly served some other, more utilitarian purpose, perhaps to hold some fishing nets together. Besides the rough, grey-black pottery, there also were a few fragments of porcelain, mostly with an ornate blue pattern on white background. From the potsherds which had originally formed part of the rim and those, which on account of their thickness, had been part of the base one could reconstruct the general shape of these pots. They were very much like the bag-shaped pots that Sydow described and the Strandloper pottery described by another dedicated amateur, Jalmar Rudner. This pottery is distinct from the pottery that I had become acquainted with in Malawi on account of its shape, decoration and finish. Whereas the so-called 'Bantu pottery' usually had well-defined necks and rims "our" bag-shaped pots lack this feature as a rule. 'Our' pots also did not display the bands of intricate geometric decoration, which adorn most of the 'Bantu pots'.

The general form of the pots found in East and Central Africa is spherical or globular while many of the pots found in Namibia are conical or bag-shaped with a distinctive pointed base. Often a thick nodule of clay protrudes from the base of 'our' pots like a pimple. The dimple that marks the pottery known as dimple-based pottery is unknown in this country. At lunchtime Helge came to see how we were getting on.

"You know I seem to remember that it wasn't far from here where I thought I had seen the bone of a human skeleton."

"Really? Did you pick it up?"

"No, I covered it with sand."

Wasn't that taking things a bit far, I wondered, but did not say anything. After all, even if I had not come, that bone would probably have been safer, buried beneath the sand here in its primary context for another few years, than on Helge's mantelpiece. With the increased interest in archaeology and the growing number of archaeology students, even remote places like this were bound to come under investigation sooner or later. The initial and most important step consisted of recording that there was material of archaeological value found in these parts of the world and I was taking that step. We now had to go beyond the question of 'Is there something?' to 'What is there?' and this question was not confined to the physical characteristics of individual specimens or artefacts, but extended to questions of human behaviour. A more discerning study of archaeological material should now lead to conclusions of what people were doing and how they were doing it. Foreign objects such as glass beads might imply contact, trade or conflict.

The attributes of single stone tools have been described, photographed, measured, drawn and talked about *ad infinitum*. Now information had to be gleaned from their association with other stone tools and from the conditions and the situations in which they were found.

"Helge, there is something white sticking up out of the ground, right there where you are standing."

I was giving the surface a close-up look. He bent down.

"That's right. That's a bone. Shall I take the sand off again?" I could not help laughing at the extremely cautious way in which he was approaching the task at hand. Before long all of us were working with hand-brooms and paintbrushes removing the sand from around the bones. Luckily the sand covering was shallow, because it would have been very difficult to make a proper trench. The bones were very white and brittle because they had been exposed to the sun, but I had glyptol with me, which quickly hardened them. We found the remains of no fewer than two human skeletons. The teeth were worn down to such an extent that we surmised that these were adults. The bones appeared to be gracile. When I held one of the thighbones next to mine, it was obvious that it must have belonged to a much shorter person than I. Whenever I did this the picture of my own skeleton flashed across my mind as I imagined it hanging up in a row with skeletons of other physical types. Mine would have been at the robust end of the continuum, with small gracile types at the other end of the scale.

The last day at Meob was spent investigating that curious, isolated pile of cobbles lying in the sand. First we took away the sand that was lying on top of the stones to see what sort of general structure one was confronted with. We were brushing and shovelling buckets full of sand. Luckily the sand was so obviously pure and sterile that we did not need to sieve enormous amounts of it. What we were exposing looked almost like a stone pavement over a tiny mound. We had been concentrating our efforts on the one end of this row of cobbles when it became obvious that we would not be able to uncover the entire occurrence with the equipment and time at our disposal.

Being under the impression that the structure was symmetrical I wanted to check this out by opening up a slice of the structure at the other end. Thus another axis was revealed, making for a T-shaped or cross-shaped arrangement. Digby, of course, wanted to see what was underneath the stones and I had to admit that I was not completely disinterested in that aspect either. Pushed by time and our gradually fading store of energy, we photographed our progress and then lifted stones within a one-metre square right on top of the heap. The sand below these stones was no different from that covering them, as was the sand further down and still further down. We dug down about a meter and a half into this sterile dune sand before we gave up.

Tired and a little disappointed we back-filled, or rather, levelled the hole, having dropped a coin in it first and placed the stones back more or less in the position in which we had found them. The only 'scientific' conclusion we managed to formulate, was that these stones could not have been deposited here in this particular way by natural forces.

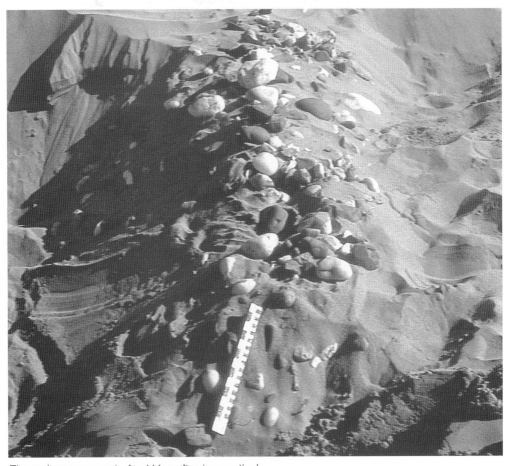

The curious pavement of cobbles after 'excavation'

CHAPTER 5

REHOBOTH

The only way in which I could tolerate the daily routine at the museum was to intersperse it with frequent field trips. The compulsory tea breaks for the sake of checking that everyone 'was at work', the surprise visits to my office to make sure that I was not working on my doctral thesis because the archaeology of Malawi was not relevant to Namibia, the lack of trust, understanding or support for what one was doing at or for the State Museum brought about a constant fear of doing, saying or thinking the wrong thing. At the best of times there was the habit of joking and of obliquely referring to ideas or events. Often these would be efforts at finding out about matters that were too sensitive to address directly.

The work in Malawi and the discovery of stone tuyères made me want to find a place where metal had been smelted and worked without making use of clay and clay tuyères. The places with traces of molten ore, which Ric Haig had found, were situated on sheer rock, eliminating the possibility of excavation. Surely at least one of the many stone tuyères which I had identified, would have been used on a surface other than bare rock? Since copper and iron were the two most likely metals to have been worked I turned my attention to areas with outcrops of native ore. That is where I would start looking for a site I could excavate.

The search for minerals and mining goes back to the ancestors of the human race. Native ores, particularly gold, silver and copper are so soft that they could be used before smelting. Obsidian was mined and traded in the middle-east because it was a sought-after material for stone tools. Bones covered with red ochre were found in the earliest formal burials. It is assumed that significance was attached to red as a colour implying abstract thought and symbolism. Presumably ochre was ground and used as colouring matter before iron ore was smelted. Iron, once smelted, proved very useful.

The Rehoboth area is exceptionally rich in a variety of minerals and there is hardly a person who cannot tell one or other intriguing story about diamond smuggling, gold digging, prospecting, mining or treasure hunting. Usually the individual who tells the story has been personally involved or knows the hero of the story.

One evening I was listening to such an account by Bodo Henckert who had been prospecting for gold in the area then known as the Rehoboth Baster Gebiet. The town of
Rehoboth in the centre of this area lies approximately 100 kilometres south of Windhoek.
The Rehoboth Basters are descended from a population of mixed origins, which escaped
colonial rule in the Cape in the mid-nineteenth century. They have been dominant in the
Rehoboth area and proudly accept and defend their identify as Rehoboth Basters in spite
of this name having been derived from a word with negative connotations.

The town is set in a striking and remarkably beautiful surrounding on the northern bank of
the Oanob River as it emerges from a canyon and penetrates the western edge of the red
Kalahari sand dunes. They are overgrown with ancient camelthorn *(Acacia erioloba)* trees,
which give the town a distinctive character. A traditional law threatens to prosecute anyone who chops down a live camelthorn tree. Several species of acacia trees in addition to
the well-known camelthorn line the banks of the Oanob River.

Ancient camelthorn trees give the town of Rehoboth a distinctive character.

According to Bodo Henckert's story, gold had been buried in one such thicket of trees, -
but all that the treasure hunters found was *copper slag*!
This was my cue. Into the laughter that the anticlimax of this story had provoked, I asked:
"But where did the copper slag come from?"
"Oh," Bodo said, still wiping the tears from his eyes and chortling.
"I don't know. They say that long ago red people who came from the rising sun, worked
copper and gold here."
This was the start of my investigations and was soon followed by a trip to Rehoboth. I met
many people who knew about the place but weren't quite sure where it was. Everyone,
however, knew someone else, who, he/she was certain, would know where the place was.
I visited farms in the area and I don't think there was one at which people did not have

either a pot or a grinding stone or some interesting piece of information, all of which allowed a little more insight into the background of this region. Stone tuyères were not unknown but no one actually possessed one.

Oom Frans Maasdorp, who became my chief guide and advisor, told me of two magnificent specimens which had been taken away by a magistrate many years ago. I took Oom Frans to the Windhoek State Museum and showed him all the tuyères I had collected so far. He said those that he had seen, which had been taken away by the magistrate, looked like those but they were not among them. But where had they been found? Near the thicket of trees behind the town. We drove to the place but Oom Frans Maasdorp was not at all sure where to start looking. I expected to find slag and he assured me that he had seen a lot of slag in the area. That was a long time ago, when he was a little boy looking after goats.

We had been walking up and down one of the red dunes, which are such a remarkable feature of the landscape here. It was hot and as the day wore on it became more and more of an effort to place one foot in front of the other. I finally collapsed on the seat of the car and when Oom Frans arrived also looking a bit wilted and dejected I said:
"Don't worry about finding it today. I'm sure we'll find it some other day. We have also achieved something by knowing that we do not need to look in this area again."
"Nooientjie" (young woman) Oom Frans said,
"when you come next time we must go and speak to Willem Dunn. He was with me very often and I am quite sure he will remember the place."

The year 1969 was a very dry one and it was depressing to drive through the farming area. There were big bare patches of hard, red, clayey soil. They looked like bits out of a gravel tennis court and were known by the name 'tennis baan'. When ground had deteriorated to the 'tennis baan' stage it was estimated to take about ten years of good rain and care before it would support grass vegetation again. There was virtually no grass left anywhere and we drove through fields of glistening stones. I wondered whether any grass seeds would remain preserved through so many drought years. Could a good rain still save the situation?

Bushes had no leaves left on them and stood with their angular black branchwork looking more like ghosts of bushes than like actual vegetation. Then one came across animals, their fur dull, with ribs and hipbones protruding. It was usual to hear farmers say that it was more economical to kill off their stock than to continue providing expensive fodder, which would eventually exceed the value of the animal.

We were approaching the Dunn's farm on a glaringly hot afternoon. The state of what used to be the garden in front of the house indicated that here water was also disappearing. I felt guilty about intruding upon a situation where obviously problems other than the prehistory of the area were occupying the minds of the people. Yet we were greeted in the most polite and friendly manner. Fresh watermelon was served, which struck me as a true miracle under the circumstances.

At first the conversation was a bit awkward but gradually an interest in the subject of the early inhabitants of the area loosened the tongues.
"You know that the area of Rehoboth is rich in minerals and here on our farm - as a matter

of fact, just beneath that tree there at the bottom of the hill — a man was shot because he had failed to keep his promise to lead two others to a pot of gold."

It was a story that Oom Frans had told on the way there.

"And long before that the people collected that silvery stuff here too," Mrs Dunn was saying,

"Yes, that we know for sure because I found two pots filled with it, just over there."

Now Mr Dunn was pointing in another direction. I couldn't quite work out what the silvery stuff was and Mr Dunn went out to fetch some. It was specularite.

"What do you think they did with it?"

"They smeared it into their hair and onto their bodies with fat," Mrs Dunn was saying,

"That is why the people were called the "vetlywe".

"Do you think they ever melted ore to make tools or weapons?"

Always more questions than answers.

Years later my friend Megan Biesele provided me with a fascinating piece of San oral literature in the form of an excerpt of a /Xam text from Bleek & Lloyd (1911). I quote in translation:

> *He takes his ochre and specularite.*
> *Specularite sparkles.*
> *So our heads are going to shimmer - because it (specularite) sparkles.*
> *They (the heads) shimmer.*
> *So the /Xam are likely to say*
> *When the old women have a talk,*
> *'That person, he is a handsome young man, because of his head which is*
> *surpassingly beautiful with the specularite's blackness.*
> *They call him '/go.'*
> *His head is very beautiful........"*

Another glimpse of that intricate and complicated picture of the past. References were limited to 'the people' or 'they'.

Oom Frans turned to Mr Dunn.

"Willem, do you remember the place behind Rehoboth where old what's-his-name found those two stones with a hole bored through them?"

Mr Dunn obviously had to turn back many pages in his book of memories. Oom Frans tried to prompt him as best he could and gradually one could see recollections assembling in his mind as his light green eyes widened and narrowed in his well-sculpted face. He was a tall, slim man and sat up straight in his chair.

"Yes, I remember now. That was where we would look after your father's goats."

Oh, my shoulder muscles relaxed. Perhaps we would find the site after all. Mr Dunn was planning a trip to town the following day and we arranged to meet mid-morning. Together the two men had reconstructed many details and were quite confident that it would not take them long to locate the place where there should still be slag and signs of burning. Once more I was meandering up and down the side of a red Kalahari sand dune with the sun beating down mercilessly upon me. Mr Dunn's son had come along as well and from the car we had spread out in a fan-like formation, walking across the area that was supposed to harbour 'my' site. The thorn bushes were high enough to screen tall figures and we had soon lost sight of one another but we could still hear one another. Mostly Mr Dunn and Oom Frans were trying to get their bearings according to the features of the landscape. There were two low-topped hills to the south of us and a fairly high blue mountain north of us and east of the town. There was a thicket of acacia trees not far from where we were and I wondered whether that was the one I had heard people talk about so often.

After some time I could not hear the voices any more, but I was sure that they would have no difficulty in letting me know very quickly if they found the site. I was getting thirsty and decided to walk back to the car in a large semi-circle branching out in a westerly direction where the other three had gone off to the east of me. Here too, there was hardly any grass left other than a few bits of hard stubble. Most of the ground was covered with red sand with a few patches of quartz gravel coming out here and there. A layer of, probably, wind blown Kalahari sand must be covering a general layer of this coarse quartz, I was thinking.

I might as well try and learn the geological conditions. I was too tired to think about what I would do should this little excursion also prove to be unsuccessful. Should I start looking for outcrops of native ore and go about systematically searching the area around those? Perhaps I should go back to the site Ric Haig had shown me near Okahandja and have a closer look at that. I was surprised to see Oom Frans at the car when I came closer and for a moment thought that they had found the place. But he just said:
"It's very hot. I came back to get some water."
I was glad of the cool-bricks in the freezer bag which were still keeping the water at a reasonable temperature and, as often in similar situations, I felt that water was the most gorgeous thirst-quenching drink there was.
"Do you think I should go and have a look on the other side?" I asked.
"Ag nooientjie," he said,
"go and look. I just don't know what is the matter with us. It must be here some place but I am getting quite confused now."
I felt awkward and did not know what to say. He took the water bottle and set off once more. I looked at my watch and was amazed that no more time had passed since the time I had last looked. I felt much like a wax candle on a very hot day and had great trouble straightening out and starting off once more. I was planning on walking a large semi-circle overlapping slightly with the one I had just completed and then I would walk ever smaller concentric semi-circles within that one.

When I started on my second concentric semi-circle my course was getting very jagged. I was simply walking from one bit of shade to the next one where I would rest and scrutinise the ground from that position in two directions: the one that I had come from and the other where I was intending to go next. The thought of lunch flashed across my mind but I rejected it immediately. The idea of fatty sandwiches was almost enough to make me ill. I had to start preparing myself for the situation that obviously was close at hand.

I could not allow my disappointment in not finding the site to show. However great my disappointment was, it did not change the fact that my new friends had given up a lot of their time and energy to help me out of the goodness of their hearts and the one thing that I had to make sure of was that they did not feel bad about it. They certainly would have preferred finding the site to not finding it. I was almost talking to myself in the desperate attempt not to let other feelings get the better of me. You can go and cry alone in your flat tonight, I told those feelings. If they were not at the car when I returned to it this time, I would drive and look for them. I still had some beer in the cool bag. We would have that and then I would go home. I was just getting into the truck when I saw a figure coming through the bush. It was Oom Frans and I went to meet him. As usual his face did not show much expression and this time I looked away before checking his eyes. I started to say something when he spoke up:

"Nooientjie, ons het hom gekry" (Young woman, we have found it).

I looked up and there was mischief in his eyes. I felt like flinging my arms around him. Something made the furrows in his weather-beaten brown face crack in different directions and his eyes became tiny slits with lights in them as he said:

"Yes, come and have a look. It's a huge place. I don't know how we managed to miss it all along."

Only then did I find my voice.

"Let me get my cameras," and we set off.

The first thing I noticed was what looked like a big hole with quite a pile of sand with stones next to it but I did not pay much attention to this because, although obvious, it did not strike me as being significant. In a radius of about 10 metres around it there were numerous concentrations with slag: green slag and black slag and some with a golden to copper colour. There were quite a few stone chips, although I did not find any retouched or secondarily worked tools. Many of the quartz cobbles looked as though they had cracked in the heat of a fire and there was a lot of charcoal around as well. There were also black schist stones and then Mr Dunn came up to me with a piece of mica schist with a high talc content.

"This is very broken but ..." he started.

"I know," I said, "I know them. It's part of a tuyère".

"Stones like this were used," he was trying to continue, "to bore holes through them."

"Look," I interrupted again, "there is still some slag on it."

"That is because it was used in the fire," he said.

Tuyere fragments

"There you can still see part of the curvature of the hole" and I slid my finger along what was left of a hole in the tuyère. When I finally wanted to offer the beers it was so late that Oom Frans suggested we go home and have some tea at his house. Strange how time had flown during the latter part of the afternoon when at lunch time I had thought that it had come to a standstill altogether. I was terribly keen to start work on this site as soon as possible.

THE DRIERIVIER EXCAVATION

As I prepared this expedition I told myself that it was too late in the year. This year was particularly hot and dry and there had not been a trace of rain. Yet it was as though I was driven by some demon. Nor did I know where to get assistants to help with the digging. Two of the technical assistants working for the museum had left. Only Frans, an Ovambo man, who had no previous experience in archaeological fieldwork, was happy to come along. As always I felt that my husband, Wade, was morally obliged to drop everything he was doing, to be at my command. Objectively I knew that this was unreasonable.

To start off, this site presented a problem: it was so large that it would have to be surveyed properly. In 1970 that required working with a theodolite. I was lucky to get my colleague, Dr Erich Wendt, to come and help me for a day. We put out strings over a grid of five metre squares over a large area. While we were doing this, another volunteer, Dr Mary Seely, who worked at the Namib Desert Research Station, became so interested in the site that she offered to help with the excavation for a while. I took that to be a lucky omen and decided to come and set up camp as soon as possible. An excavation would require full-time on-the-spot presence for a least a week or two.

Where would the prehistoric smiths have set up their camp? The 'red people' who were said to have come from the east, how did they come and why? And who called them the 'red people'? Those who gave them that name, presumably, were not red themselves. Black Damara or yellow San? Well, these questions were the reasons why I was doing the work I was busy with. But which questions were the appropriate ones to ask? I needed to find reasonable questions to ask, that would have a chance of being answered by the discoveries we might be making here.

Archaeologists have found skeletal remains indicating age, sex, and height of an individual. An analysis of the bone could even tell whether they had eaten wild plants or cultivated crops or whether they were healthy human beings or whether they had suffered stress and strain. But skin colour, hair texture or shape and colour of the eyes could not be reconstructed. Nor can skeletons tell you anything about the language they spoke when they were alive and well. Or to which gods they prayed and which songs they sang.

We decided on a campsite on the edge of the thicket of trees, which on closer inspection was not all that thick. It gave that impression from a distance because the acacia trees have a large brushwork of branches. On the ground the individual stems of the trees were fairly far apart. I had brought long boards and trestles, which provided a lot of table space and these were put up under a big tree. Two small tents were pitched fairly quickly and we made off to the site, which was a five-minute walk away. First of all I was going to map the various concentrations of slag and charcoal. There were quite a few of them and near each one there were a few large black stones. We called them hearthstones because they lay close together and reminded one of a few stones put in a fire to support a pot or grid.

The sky was overcast and the air very still when I became aware of a far off noise. Frans was standing up straight and looking over to the west as though he had seen something of great interest there. I followed his look and saw a murky reddish wall of dust approaching. A sandstorm. A few branches were moving slightly and then there was stillness again.

"Mary, there is a sandstorm approaching. Cover your face with your scarf and kneel down with your head in your lap when it comes close."

We were all three rushing to put heavy stones on the various items that might blow away. The storm was upon us before we could do much. Sand grains were beating against arms and legs like lashings from a whip. The force of the wind was such that one automatically lowered one's weight to the ground and closed one's eyes. I just hoped that my handbag with notebook would stay secure. The scraggly branches of the bushes were being torn at as though some mighty force was grabbing them in an effort to uproot them. And then, almost as suddenly as it had started, the happening was over. The sky in the west was clear. A few rays of the setting sun were lighting up the drought-stricken scene and the air was still once more. We strung out a few more metres of string so that we could start mapping early the next day and then took the things we wanted in the camp and set off for a well-deserved rest.

The sight that met us where we had set up our camp earlier on can only be described as one of destruction. The ground was swept clean of all tracks or foot marks as though no one had been there for years. The little igloo tent was blown against a bush and hung there like a stray piece of laundry. Mary's one-person stick-up tent had rolled away and was lying on its side about 100 metres from where we had put it up. Chairs had collapsed and were blown over. The table-top was resting against the trunk of the nearby tree and the trestles stood like orphans. Cups, mugs, plates and cutlery were strewn around carelessly. I stood there for a few minutes and took in the sight of our sand-coated belongings. How many more times was this going to happen? Sandstorms of this sort turned out to be

The area was marked by several concentrations of slag, charcoal, split cobbles and sand discoloured from heat (Photo W. Pendleton)

a daily event. They were, however, fairly localised and a few times we saw them passing us at a distance of a few hundred metres. Towards the end of my stay I knew them so well that I could judge fairly accurately whether they were going to pass by or to hit us full-force.

When we had plotted the first concentration of slag, charcoal, split cobbles and discoloured sand we started to excavate. Frans did most of the excavating, that is horizontally brushing loose earth into little heaps in the demarcated squares and moving the deposit from there into buckets to where the excavated material would be sifted. Mary and I did the rest of the plotting onto graph paper. In the process of doing this, my attention became more fixed on that shallow depression in the ground with the pile of loose material next to it that formed a central point on our big map of graph paper. As the excavation of the slag concentration was not exposing any definite pattern or structure, I was considering turning to this hole.

The pit furnace cleared with fragments of anvil stones on one side

We would start work well before sunrise. By about ten in the morning the production curve would start dropping and one would take refuge in the shade of the low bushes more and more frequently. The work results between 12:00 and 15:00 did just not warrant the will power necessary to achieve them. It was December, the hottest month of the year. I was convinced of that! Between 12:00 and 15:00 we would rest in camp or we would go to Oom

Frans Maasdorp's house or Bodo Henckert's and take a shower. Oom Frans' wife would serve us hot tea, which was wonderfully refreshing. The day before Mary was due to leave I must have seemed depressed. She had promised to send Wade out but I knew that he had enough of his own work to do and could not leave for longer than a few hours at a time.

"What is it?" Mrs Maasdorp asked, looking at me with her big brown eyes.

She did not spend any time on pretences.

"Tomorrow I will be out there alone with Frans," I said and the expression on my face probably said the rest.

"You must get some help," she said.

I just shrugged my shoulders.

"Perhaps my husband will come out tomorrow evening." I said.

"That's nice. Tell him to come by here and I will have some fresh meat for him."

"Oh, then please come out with him and we'll have a nice fire and a braai."

"O.K. we can do that. What about Raymond?"

"You must bring him of course." Raymond was her son, 12 or 13 years of age.

"I don't mean for the braai. Couldn't he help you with the work?"

"If he could come that would be marvellous." I meant it most sincerely.

"The holidays have just started and he would love it. And then I suggest that you go to Drotski's farm. Raymond can show you the way. There is a man who, I am sure, would come and help you, if you could just pay him a little bit of money. His family are very poor and when he was in here the other day he was saying that he's prepared to do almost anything for just a little bit of cash. The only problem is that he cannot leave his wife and the little children alone on the farm for too long."

I looked at Mrs Maasdorp and thought what a wonderful woman Oom Frans had for a wife. Nine children, of whom she had lost two, and hard work in the family's butcher shop, had given her serious character a depth and a greatness that I could only marvel at.

The next day Frans and I were alone. I did most of the brushing and labelling of the artefacts while Frans carried the heavy buckets and did a lot of shovelling.

"What's the matter?" I asked when I saw him vigorously beating the ground with his shovel at one point.

"Come and look" he said, "a big scorpion."

It was indeed an extraordinary big, black scorpion.

I couldn't face the thought of Wade not coming that evening and kept on looking down the road and listening for the noise of our car. At last there were two cars: Wade's followed by the Maasdorp's car. When I saw two people in the car with Wade I thought he had brought Raymond Maasdorp along but it was yet another helper. It was a young boy who had been to the museum before and was very interested in archaeology. Wade had met him in Windhoek and on the spur of the moment he had decided to come out and help with the excavation. Wilfried Böhm and Raymond got on very well together and were a real tonic through the days of that hot, sandstorm-stricken, scorpion-infested excavation.

The highlights were the fires we had in the evening, particularly when there was fresh meat to roast on the coals. So we were sitting around the fire that evening and waiting for the hard wood to burn down a little when Raymond Maasdorp suddenly jumped up with a cry. Wilfried also had jumped up and was vigorously stamping on .... a scorpion.

"Good work, Wilfried," he was praised from all sides. And we told how Frans had killed a huge black brute at the site that morning. As I was talking I noticed something moving under Wade's chair.

"Lift your leg" I shouted. As he did so a scorpion dashed out from beneath his chair as though it was making for the fire, but turned when it came close to the edge of the fire and darted off in another direction. There was shouting and screaming and then Wade said: "I think I've got him."
"Raymond, go and put on your shoes." Mrs Maasdorp was saying.
"That's two scorpions within less than ten minutes." Wilfried was observing.

Wade had gone to check that the tent was zipped up and I decided to let the two boys sleep in the back of the truck. We had barely settled down again, somewhat uneasily, when Mrs Maasdorp let out a cry and then I lost track of who saw which one next. We killed 15 scorpions within the next 50 minutes. I don't know how we did it, but we managed to see humour in the situation and these poisonous arachninds were all killed amid shrieks of fright as well as laughter, although we knew very well that these scorpion stings were not only painful but could cause death.
As we were tidying up everybody carefully shone their torches around everything they intended to pick up and everywhere they were going.
"Don't you think it's time to call it quits and just leave this horrible place?" Wade said to me under his breath.
That had just not occurred to me. How could I do that without having found the furnace or any indication of where all the slag came from? But I could not endanger my helpers, particularly the two boys.
"I'll go in to see the doctor tomorrow and ask him what I should do in case someone does get stung by a scorpion," I said.
"That is the least you can do."

Wade had to leave again at five the next morning, but promised to come out again in the evening with more cold beer and lemonade. That day was l00% better than the previous one. Instead of two we now were four and went off to fetch a fifth helper from the nearby farm that Mrs Maasdorp had mentioned. Izak immediately agreed to help us.

We started clearing the depression in the centre of the work area. There were branches, twigs, leaves and dust in and around it. Once all this had been cleared away and the surface was carefully brushed with hand brooms and paint brushes, a much more symmetrical structure could be observed than before. There was an oval, flat bottom to a hole that extended down into the natural layer of coarse quartz for about 50 centimetres. Three of the sides to this hole were fairly steep. The fourth one looked as though it had been somewhat disturbed. Concentrating on this area more thoroughly, I now noticed that a few of those odd angular rocks I had called hearthstones in the other places were also lying on one pile of loose material that had been heaped up on the side of the hole. They presented a puzzle I simply had to work out. I went from one assortment of these 'hearth stones' to the next, photographing each lot. I swept the surface around them, put my scale down and took a photograph, allowing frowns reflecting a wondering and wandering mind, to crease my forehead. Some of the surfaces were flat and apparently worn fairly smooth.

Then something clicked. It was not my camera. In my mind I suddenly saw the different fragments moving towards each other and fitting tightly into each other. I put down my camera and tried to put this thought into action. It worked. The different fragments had once been part of a big stone with a flat surface.
"So what?" I asked myself.

"What could big flat stones have been used for at a place where metal was being worked?" Anvils.

I could see the different fragments fitting together

That was the only answer I could come up with. I was dying for the hours to pass so that I could hear what Wade would have to say about that. I showed the boys and Frans and Izak. When I went in to Rehoboth I asked them to see whether they could fit the ones that I had not yet tried fitting together.

The anti-scorpion campaign, Raymond left and Wilfried right

The doctor in Rehoboth was very sympathetic when I told him about our scorpion plague but he advised me not to use anti-serum because it was so easy to give an overdose. The best would be to simply put whoever had been stung on the back of the truck and bring them straight to him. At least I would know what to do.

When I came back and told the boys what the doctor had said they suggested that we try and influence the scorpions not to come to our camp in the first place. I thought that was a very good idea.

"Why not put up a sign?" I suggested.

"Yes. We'll say: Scorpions not wanted here."

"No," Wilfried improved on it "We'll say: scorpions will be prosecuted."

"In all three languages" Raymond added.

We laughed and joked about it but did not do anything until we had another invasion that evening around the fire. The next morning Raymond and Wilfried got down to business and fabricated a signboard. I approved. It would be good for the morale, if nothing else. But that evening there were three more scorpions. We had overlooked that the sign was far too high up on the trunk of the tree for the scorpions to read. So we lowered it and luckily no more scorpions molested us after that.

One afternoon I suggested a little diversion in the form of a walk over to the two little kopjes south of the site.

"No," Izak said, "Don't go there. That place is known as the home of the puffadders. I didn't want to say anything before now because you are camped so close to that horrible place but please don't go and ask for trouble."

We stayed and continued with the work of excavating the area around the hole.

We started clearing the depression in the centre of the work area

I had put down a base line along the long axis of the hole. We were taking away the loose material that was darkened from heat and which I think must have been filling in the hole.

71

About 40 centimetres below the original surface two furrows were starting to take shape as we brushed away the very fine sand and dust that filled them. In the one, two larger fragments of stone were lying and one piece of mica schist was lying in the other one. I left them in place and photographed them before picking them up. What a thrill to turn them over and discover that they were tuyère fragments.

We had also found a couple of tuyère fragments in the course of plotting the concentration of split pebbles, charcoal and slag that was situated a few metres away from what I now started to see as the furnace in the centre of a large working area. We had no single undamaged tuyère but eleven fragments. I was satisfied with that evidence. Pottery finds were limited to minute undecorated bodysherds which had been picked up on the surface. One could not deduce much from that. They might have been dropped here hundreds of years before the site was ever worked or hundreds of years later. But there was still some digging to be done. I wanted to make sure that the side where we had found the tuyère fragments and which had looked as though it had been disturbed from the start, was really the only side from which the furnace fire had been fed. Consequently I dissected the hole once more at right angles to the original baseline. We took away more of the loose sandy surface layer and the quartz gravel beneath. It was in this quartz gravel, approximately 50 centimetres from the surface and only about 30 centimetres from the edge of the furnace hole that we came across that wonderfully unambiguous bit of evidence: a large sherd from a beaker-shaped clay pot, with a double row of fingernail impressions decorating the pot around the opening.

A large sherd from a beaker-shaped pot about 20 cm across

The stone tuyère project was starting to take on a number of definitive characteristics. The people working metal with stone tuyères were very stone oriented. They used stone to make their tuyères and used stone anvils. Apparently they used a very simple but nonetheless effective method of open-pit smelting. And their relationship to clay? They knew about clay and used clay pots but they did not use clay for tuyères or for the making of furnaces. This was an extremely important point because it negated the introduction of metal-working by Bantu-speakers.

Surely, if a stone tuyère person had seen or even only heard about metal being worked in a furnace with bellows, which were connected to the fire with tuyères made of clay he/she would have imitated them! Had he/she not known clay he/she might have tried to duplicate a clay tuyère with stone, but the large potsherd found in that primary context and now confirming the surface finds of sherds, indicated that clay was not only known but also used. The question arising out of this is whether we have here in Namibia a separate and independent development of metalworking.

Three radio carbon samples provided dates placing the operations at the Drierivier site into the middle of the seventeenth century. This made it unlikely that the arrival of Jan van Riebeeck in 1652 at the Cape of Good Hope could have had any influence on the developments of copper working in the Rehoboth area. By that time Bantu-speaking peoples had already settled along the Kavango River. So far, however, there is no evidence for Bantu speakers having lived further south or for having had contact with non-Bantu speaking people living to the south.

The work at Drierivier raised many questions. They touched on the evolution of our techno-society, on the origins of specialization and urbanization. Imagine seeing all present day cultures as the foliage on a two-pronged tree of cultural evolution. The techno-societies represent the foliage on the end of the one thick branch of that tree and the hunter-gatherer societies represent the foliage on the end of the other branch. What marked the fork in the original trunk of the tree? Did the inventions of metalworking, pottery and the domestication of plants and animals lead to urbanization, industrialization and large-scale societies with all their glory and doom?

Or did similar inventions accompany an otherwise non-material development as well? What about the Meso-American cultures of the Maya and the Inca? There was monumental architecture and there were highly developed forms of art – even in the absence of a discovery of the wheel! There were rituals of extreme cruelty, like the sacrifice of still-beating hearts of virgins but no indication of warfare!
Could we learn from these developments?
How could knowledge of these different developments aid us in the solution of the problems facing us today?

Answers to these questions require lifetimes of work and faith and vision that exceed the capacity of most individual minds. The exciting thing about our day and age is the ever-increasing number of workers and fields of knowledge that are being investigated. The speed that accompanies all other developments at a cumulative rate also marks the growth of understanding and awareness that is the only hope we have in our struggle to continue as a species on this earth.

Africa. I had approached my Professor of African Art, William Bascom and pointed out:
"But people in Namibia and Angola do carve!"
He replied: "Yes, there is that one piece here that Edwin Loeb brought back from his expedition in 1948, but nobody knows what it is."

Edwin Loeb had died and his wife could not remember details relating to the large cylindrical wooden body, which was covered with faces carved onto it. I was very familiar with the style of the carved faces. Such portraits adorned round wooden stools commonly found in Namibian homes. Similar wooden masks decorated the walls of many houses. These woodcarvings were generally referred to as Owambo carvings, and more recently, facetiously - as Adenauer faces - because of a perceived similarity to the triangular shaped face of Konrad Adenauer, the first West-German Chancellor after World War II.

These beautiful stools were known as Ovambo carvings with Adenauer faces

During the course I took with Professor William Bascom, well-known expert on the art of West Africa, he once said:
"'Beatrice, you'll have to go and colour in that large empty spot on the art map of Africa.'"

Professor Nelson Graburn, teaching Art and Folklore in Berkeley, was studying art among the Eskimo and had put forward the theory that art was used and could be used as a medium of communication between people of different cultures. This role would be particularly significant in the case of contact between technologically superior people and people with a less advanced material culture. This situation repeats itself all over the world. Because art has to do with status in most western cultures, people are inclined to attach prestige value to art in other cultures as well. Often, however, it must be declared as art before the masses will accept it as such. Once a market is created, artists want to explore and exploit the potential. They are successful if they manage to communicate.

It would be so interesting to know more about how that final wave of Bantu-speaking peoples had come to settle here. The recent arrival of the immigrant groups might be reconstructed with the aid of oral tradition but there were the Kavango groups who had already been living in the area for a long time.

Thinking about this project, I once more deeply regretted that Wade could not have come along and been part of it. We could have worked together beautifully. He could have concentrated on the ethnographic background and I could have delved into the archaeological work. I could not help thinking about the possibility of his being appointed to the museum staff as well, once he had his doctoral degree.

But I had to shake off these thoughts. I tried to get into the right frame of mind to meet a missionary who had sent potsherds to the museum. He had found them while excavating the foundations for his house near Kapako. He had apparently struck an occupation horizon well below the surface. He showed us the clay pot he had found. It was broken but one could see the typical spherical shape with a clearly defined neck and a well-worked rim around the opening. The walls of the missionary's house were by now almost to the height of the roof so that there was no chance of looking at the profiles of the foundation for more material. But the pit for the sewer (which was not yet in use) was still there. At about 50 centimetres from the surface there were potsherds and a piece of bone sticking out of the wall of this hole. We laid out a test square on the surface and recovered a small sample of material. I went around looking for more exposures to see how far this horizon extended. A refuse pit a few hundred metres from the house provided another profile and again there were some potsherds protruding from the sidewall at some depth below the surface.

A watu - or canoe - is cut out of a single huge tree trunk

We had pitched our camp at Kapako, less than a kilometre upstream from the missionary's house, on the edge of the steep, high riverbank, which presented another opportunity of looking beneath the surface.

I hired a watu and had myself rowed to get a look at the section of the riverbank rising above the level of the water. It was not easy to see but I could make out pottery and even stone artefacts protruding from the profile. Several beautifully made Early Stone Age artefacts from the Kavango region had been brought to the museum from time to time. I gasped as I imagined the possibility of an excavation exposing layers with cultural material dating back to Early Stone Age times – two to three million years ago. Vast spans of hunter-gatherer history, possibly predecessors of *Homo sapiens*..... in the cradle of humanity ..... my imagination was in over-drive.

I was to work on the Iron Age. It was the beginning of the Iron Age that I was so interested in. Metal work and pottery together with sedentary habitation and domesticated plants and animals were part of the syndrome marking the transition from the Stone Age to the Iron Age. That was my fascination. It was so easy to get lost in the details. No, I did not expect to discover the origins of the Iron Age here at the Kavango.

Early Iron Age sites had been documented from other parts of Africa. After all, I had reported on the site at Phopo Hill in Malawi dated to approximately 300 A.D! Now I should find out how and when the information about the discoveries of pottery, metal and domesticated plants and animals had travelled to this part of the world.

I was convinced that we would hit the cultural layer, which had been noticed by the missionary while he was building his house, if we were to dig a test square close to the riverbank. I chose a site at Kapako, a stone's throw from where we had camped. My assistant, who had been trained by Rona MacCalman, was an expert at excavating and we worked quickly and efficiently through the surface layers with some cultural material: potsherds, charcoal, slag, bone and isolated fragments of stone. There was enough bone to keep a zoologist busy for quite some time. Would domestic animals be represented in the inventory of food remains which we were finding here?

The potsherds resembled those found near the missionary's house. They were not very weathered and I realised that a survey of the existing pottery in this area would be needed for comparison. Whatever the date of the excavated material might be, it would be meaningless if it could not be related to present material. At least it should be possible to say whether it was the same or different. There was not much pottery around any more and this probably was the last chance of getting a record of the final phase of traditional ceramics in the Kavango area.

'But how do you think you are going to handle another full-time project?' I asked myself. Little did I realise then that such questions were going to mark the rest of my life. There were so many critically important tasks well beyond my means of time and energy. If I could not deal with them, information would be lost forever. The result was that one could not carry out assignments as conscientiously as ought to have been the case. Or as a dear friend put it: if something is worth doing it is worth doing it badly!

I knew exactly how Wade would have reacted to my suggestion of also doing the ethnography of the Kavango pottery in addition to my archaeological work:
'Yes my dear, that is another full time project but you cannot take that on as well because you know too well how it ought to be done. You must get reliable data on who made the pot, who used it and how it was made or else you might just as well not tear the pots out of their context anyway.'
'I know', I sighed and thought of the contradictions I had already encountered in brief references to pottery in the literature and in remarks by informants. In Bantu-speaking Africa, it was generally accepted that pot-making was women's work and it was not considered an especially sacred process. In Malawi I had filmed the whole pot-making

procedure from the collecting of the clay down to the firing of the pot. Although only women had been involved in the process, there was nothing secret or sacred about it.

A woman in Malawi in the process of making a clay pot

Children would come and watch and other household chores would be done alongside. In A.C. Lawton's book on Bantu pottery a few differences in the making of pots by the Ambo (or Ovambo) and the Kavango groups are mentioned. Wambo women wait for the full moon and withdraw to the seclusion of subterranean huts to make their pots. Among the Sambiu on the banks of the Kavango, men were the potters, not women. The records of Viereck and Sydow on pot-making in the central parts of the country also mentioned

Kudumo, a Sambiu man in the process of making clay pots

men. This was a point that would require careful investigation. I revised my timetable and scheduled us to get up half an hour earlier in the morning. Each day I made a packed lunch, which I was going to eat while I was driving to the different villages to collect pots. I repaired the gas lamp so that I could work up my notes in the evenings after dark. The two assistants had to take over all kitchen duties. I abandoned the habit of washing my clothes every second day in favour of gaining an extra bit of sleep. Subconsciously I was struggling with the conflict of doing all this work, which was only indirectly related to my main interest: metal smelting without the use of clay. I felt that I should have continued with my investigations of stone tuyère sites in the vicinity of Windhoek. The archaeology of Namibia, as I saw it, was that of the arid and semi-arid parts of the country, which had traditionally been occupied by hunter-gatherers, presumably the ancestors of the present day Khoe, San and Damara.

My work in the area along our northern border should merely serve to illustrate the contrast in cultures of people living in different environments. I had to rationalise how the work I had been directed to do would complement the main thrust of my research on the prehistory of those cultures, which did not fit into the general Iron Age image of southern Africa. I was utterly fascinated by everything I saw and learned. This stimulation gave me energy. At the same time there was the fear of getting sidetracked. I was afraid of losing sight of my main aim and goal. Or what I thought my main aim and goal ought to be.
'And with that,' I heard a frustrated little voice of conscience saying, 'you will continue to get ever more involved in other interesting things such as your wood-carving.'
'But don't you think that's relevant?' I countered, talking to my other self.
'Of course it is,' and again there was the quality of Wade's voice.
'To see art as a means of communication between two different cultures, particularly in this country, would be of tremendous importance.'
'You see, then how can I not do it? Your American training has messed me up!' I was on the defensive.
'By teaching you too much?' I could see the amusement in his eyes.
Feeling sorry for myself I wished he were there to help me. These soliloquies were conducted when I went on the afternoon collecting trips. I had designed a simple questionnaire for the contacts with potters and carvers. In this way a number of differences between the immigrant groups from Angola and the local Kavango groups could be observed. I acquired pots and carvings with the relevant information of who had made them, where they were collected and with what aim in mind they had been made.

Working in the pit at Kapako the finds were diminishing as we went down. At a depth of less than a metre from the surface we were again finding pottery. But it looked very different from what we had found earlier on. It was badly weathered and small fragments of ceramic ware crumbled when touched. I was brushing away the soil very gently when the outline of a large sherd emerged. The edge of the rim appeared to be intact and a good part of the body of the pot seemed unbroken. As I was brushing away the ground from a gently hollow or concave shape it became clear that the inside of the vessel was facing upwards. The plain surface looked like one big crack and picking it up would have left us with no more than a few handfuls of ceramic crumbs. We poured glyptol over it and left it to dry *in situ* overnight. To our delight it had hardened by the next day and we could pick up a large piece of clay pot. The outside of the pot was prettily decorated with a broad band of geometric impressions below a well-formed rim and gently shaped neck typical of an Iron Age pot. This find was treated with the respect worthy of crown jewels. We felt doubly rewarded for the trouble we had taken when the charcoal, which had been collected for dating in the same layer as this potsherd, indicated an age of well over 1,000 years. This early date for the Iron Age demanded further work. Kapako in Southwestern Africa was 500 years younger than Phopo in Malawi in East Africa.

THE GREAT WOOD CARVERS OF KAVANGO

During my second expedition to the Kavango I had taken on the task of collecting information for a chapter in a book, which Nelson Graburn was going to publish "Ethnic and Tourist Arts". I witnessed a number of interesting buying and selling scenes on the weekly market installed by the government at Rundu and at some of the stands along the road. Markets and trading provide opportunities for cross-cultural understanding. This might promote economic, social and political transition. Here contact was being promoted via the medium of art between an industrialised large scale society and a peasant society. Might a similar phenomenon have taken place in prehistoric times between a mobile hunter-gatherer society and a sedentary, technologically more advanced agricultural society?

At the weekly Rundu market carvers were lining up to sell their work

The state-owned "Bantu Beleggings Korporasie (BBK)" (Bantu Investment Corporation) was obviously aware of the world market that existed for so-called primitive or non-western art. Every Friday a number of officials in Rundu, the capital of the region, would set up shop in front of a large shed in which the carvings they bought were stored. The carvers or their friends or relatives would come from near and far and line up in a long queue with what they were going to offer for sale. People living two or three days walk away from Rundu would come to that market. Many of them came from across the river in Angola where there were no good roads connecting them to towns or centres in other parts of Angola.

Several carvers living in villages along the well-made gravel road that ran parallel to the Kavango thus linking up this territory with the rest of Namibia, did however, not go to the Friday market. When I asked them why they did not go to the Friday market they said that they could get better prices for their products by the side of the road. An average of three to four cars would pass the village every day and many of them would stop when they saw the carvings lining the road. Most of the people who bought the carvings were white although blacks also bought carvings. During the sixties and seventies the areas along Namibia's northern border were virtually inaccessible to anyone other than government employees and their next of kin. Tourism was not yet known. The political philosophy behind this had been demonstrated painfully well by Wade, who in spite of being my husband, had not been allowed to accompany me. Nevertheless, the government officials had, inadvertently, initiated an incipient kind of trade. They would buy or barter carvings and ethnographic items to take to Windhoek or to other towns for curio dealers and/or give them as gifts to family and friends.

Other than that, carvings could only be obtained from the BBK. Part of the stock was available to dealers in Namibia and South Africa while the remainder would go to markets in Europe and America. As far as I knew this was the only source for carvings from the Kavango for the world market. With that in mind, it was odd watching officials, who were neither art connoisseurs, art historians, art critics nor artists in their own right, evaluate and appraise the work of the local carvers. Yet they judged and bought up an enormous amount of material. I seemed to understand from the people selling, that they could always make something that the officials would buy, even if they did not pay much. In this way the officials could be seen as an indirect market force influencing production which the buyers on the open market might not have approved of at all.

Standing in line, waiting for his turn at the table where the officials concluded the buying transactions, a man was absent-mindedly handling a large wooden figure. It looked as though it was wearing a long suit or cloak and a tall, pointed hood. Puzzled at first, I suddenly recognised the mask and dress of a Chokwe dancer, which I had seen in a film in which figures like this were approaching the village square through the tall grass of the savannah. I could not remember whether the occasion had been a harvest festival or an initiation ceremony.

I was right in assuming that the carver was Kachokwe. This figure to him must have been as familiar as the figure of a priest in his robes, or a judge in his tunic, to us. With his carving he had given expression of something that was important and valuable in his culture. I was thinking of the multitude of representations of a cross or the Virgin Mary in our culture. Some whites, probably relatives of people working at Rundu, who were visiting, were wandering along the line of people with their work and stopped to look at the hooded figure. They asked how much he wanted for it, but shook their heads when he named a price.

The man was obviously getting nervous and I dreaded the encounter at the table because I doubted that the figure would mean much to the official buyers. A man came by whom I had briefly met at the Post Office the previous day. He picked up the figure and said something to the carver in his native language. The carver nodded and the man left. There were about another ten people ahead of him in the line. When there were but two to go, he took his carving and left the line. I watched him cross the road and pass the line of houses in which the white officials at Rundu were living. At the Post Office he turned right and I suddenly had the idea that he might go to the house of the man who had talked to him earlier on. I got into the car and followed. Sure enough, there he was standing on the veranda of a house and knocking on the door. My acquaintance from the Post Office opened.

On the spur of the moment I got out of the car, walked up to them, introduced myself and simply said that I was so very interested in the figure and wanted to know what was going to happen to it. Mr Hoehn was very friendly, saying, that of course, he knew who I was because visitors did not go unnoticed in a small place like Rundu. We were soon involved in a most interesting conversation. Mr Hoehn had been living along the Okavango for

some years and had developed a sincere interest in the carving done by the local people. He was a mine of information and had a remarkable collection of very interesting work.

"This tall hooded figure," he was saying, "is the sort of unusual thing that I like to go for. It is very well-carved. Have a look at it - but because people don't know what it means, they don't buy it."

He had put his finger on it. What was a well-known symbol or item of value in the one culture was foreign to the other culture and therefore did not communicate itself.

"You should see the things people buy like crazy," he was continuing,

"The other day there was a group of young army recruits at the market. They practically tore the carvings away from the one guy. What had he carved? - little stickmen in uniforms carrying guns." He laughed.

"You wouldn't believe it, they were but poorly cut pieces of wood — but these guys just went beserk and even ordered more - and a piece of art like this here..."

He was looking admiringly at the figure he had just bought.

"A beautiful piece of work - and they don't see it. I don't care if I don't know what it means, but I can recognise a good piece of work."

I was surprised at how well he had illustrated the point I had been belabouring in my mind for some time now. Communication was brought about by either selling works of art that represented a value in one's own culture or, by recognising an item of value in another culture and representing that. If that other value was acknowledged and recognised - like the little wooden soldiers with guns - then it would be accepted or even desired - and thereby the process of communication would have come full circle.

"Look at this piece." Mr Hoehn was now showing me his collection.

"Can you see what this is — I mean do you see what it's supposed to be?"

It stood about 50 centimetres from the ground and looked like a bowl on a stem. Something about it looked familiar but I could not place it. It was very smooth and the wood had been polished to a golden sheen.

One carving portrayed a Chokwe dancer in full costume, 75 cm high

"You do not see it," he said almost triumphantly.

"It took me a couple of close looks, but then I knew, but I also

86

knew no-one else would see it. You see, I know these people quite well by now. Their minds don't work like ours, but I am starting to understand them. That is also why I want to learn their language. And I am going to learn it, too. I can make myself understood quite easily but that isn't enough. I want to really talk to them, to find out how their minds work. You still don't know what that bowl represents, do you?"

He was obviously savouring my inability to identify the carving.

"When I bought that, it was the same as with the figure this morning. I always go to the market on Fridays to see what they bring. I always give them a chance to sell the things for the highest price they can get. Like this morning, when I came there and saw the figure, I went to the man and told him what I would pay if he couldn't sell it to anyone else. I know them well enough by now. I knew this morning he was not going to sell it, as soon as I saw it. Because the government guys - ha - they don't pay much for things like this. They want the little carved ashtrays and rubbish like that. You see, they have to think of what tourists will buy, people at airports and so on. And they are not going to carry large bag drums or things like that, so they make the little masks and that - those are not really native things. No native uses a little mask like that and that I am not interested in. I want to have those things that are really part of them...."

"Is this bowl part of their culture?" I cut in.

"Oh, that bowl - you don't realise what it is, do you? Well, think of the church - do you know - when you go to communion - do you get it? The chalice! The nicely polished brass chalice!? That's what it is. When the priest holds it in front of your face as he administers the holy communion you see your own reflection. That is what those carved faces on the wooden cup imply. That is how you can see yourself like in a mirror in that shiny metal cup. Do you see it now? But because it is out of proportion and in another medium - we are not used to having it portrayed like that, which is why it appears foreign to us. Do you know what I paid for that? *R3.00,* that's nothing for a carving like that. It's even hard to find a piece of wood that size, these days. It's just as well the BBK chaps don't want large carvings, because even if they wanted them, they wouldn't be able to find them because all the old trees are cut down and they take a long time to grow, these dolf-wood (kiaat) trees." (*Pterocarpus angolensis*)

I wished I had brought a tape recorder to get all the valuable information that was just pouring out of this man. I was glad that he did not seem to be in any great hurry to go anywhere and was happy to continue talking.

"It's not that they don't realise this, the BBK. They are not stupid and they have got eyes to see. They notice how the dolf-wood trees are disappearing so they are starting a saw mill here. They are going to bring in wood and they will get pieces cut and the natives can then just come here and get their raw material in blocks. You see, they are interested in keeping this carving going because they want the money. Not for themselves. All the profit they make on these carvings comes straight back here and helps with the development of the area. I believe the carvings themselves have already paid for this saw mill. You can't expect them to understand anything about art. That's not their business. They are practical people but that is why I keep my eyes open. Because soon one won't be able to get these unusual pieces any more. Because, you see, the carvers are also not stupid. They understand what sells and what doesn't. They don't carve for pleasure. They want to make money like everyone else. There is one chap here, who makes chairs - these chairs that you are sitting on."

Actually, I had noticed the furniture as I had entered the room. They were handsomely carved wooden chairs, which were, contrary to my expectation, extremely comfortable. "Well, I tell you," Mr Hoehn was carrying on, "that guy has the makings of an industry there. Those chairs are a good piece of handiwork and do you know what I paid for them? R12,00. Man, I couldn't even buy the wood for that price. It takes a long time but I don't care. I can wait. It's worth it, because they are so well-made by hand."

I asked whether I could photograph some of the items in his collection.

"But of course."

We arranged that I would come back the following afternoon to photograph them in the light of the setting sun.

THE SAN AND THE IRON AGE

I had to get back to the excavation. This time I was working east of Rundu, at Uvunguvungu or Vungu Vungu, according to the map, a place named after the sausage tree (*Kigelia africana*). It was rather a stunted specimen of a tree and when I remarked on this I was told why: the first Sambiu who came to settle here had brought that particular tree here from the east. These trees were not really at home here, I was told and that was why this one did not look too healthy. I did not, in fact, notice a single sausage tree west of Vungu Vungu. But I did not look too carefully.

Vungu Vungu is a place named after the sausage tree planted there, (in the background), by the first Sambiu chieftainess

At any rate I thought that it would be worth looking for signs of past occupation around a fabled place like this, because it was also said that the first Chieftainess of the Sambiu had put up her residential enclosure close to the Vungu Vungu tree. Now there was a maize field here. The present owners had been small children when they came here but they could remember clearing the thick bush for cultivation. Would they tell their children about this? It would be such precious information for a collection of oral tradition. The maize field now stretched down to the edge of the river. This year's crop had been har-vested so we could walk up and down the cultivated furrows looking for artefacts.

Indeed, we did find them. I thought that some of them could well have been ploughed up and might originally have been at least 25 to 50 centimetres below the surface. I laid out a large grid and began by testing every second square in a trench 15 metres long. One end of the trench terminated in a little gully that led down to the river. We found a good number of potsherds, bone, metal fragments and what appeared to be remnants of the floor of a clay hut. The potsherds resembled those found in the upper layer at Kapako. They were not badly weathered and were marked by similar patterns of decoration around the rims and necks of the pots. Probably they were not very old.

Oddly enough, we also found a few chipped stones and ostrich eggshell beads. When remarking upon this to one of the local workers I had again hired to help with the digging, he said quite matter-of-factly:
"Yes, these are Bushmen things."
"But I thought the Vungu Vungu tree was planted by a Sambiu chief?" I asked.
"Yes, that's right," he said, "but there are always Bushmen with Sambiu people".
When the archaeologist in me hears statements with 'always' or 'forever', I want to en-quire "when did 'always' or 'forever' start?" In this case charcoal samples, which were submitted for carbon 14 dating started giving an answer to this question. According to the charcoal samples, the material we were excavating here was dated to approximately 1650 A.D. It could therefore be assumed that Bantu speaking peoples as well as San had been living here over three hundred years ago. Had the Vungu Vungu tree been planted here that long ago?

On one of my visits to the Kavango I had come across an arrangement which seemed to be quite common in this area. For part of the year, San families joined up with Bantu families. They pitched their grass shelters or windbreaks a few hundred metres beyond the stockaded enclosure of the Bantu homestead and looked after the cattle for the Bantu. They would have 'veldkos' (wild plant food) to exchange for meat. After the rainy season had begun the San families would leave again.

Once, just at the beginning of the dry season, I came to a kraal near Mbundza where a San group had just arrived to stay for the next few months. The Mbundza family warmly welcomed them. The children of the hosts as well as of the arrivals were obviously delighted and shrieking with joy to see one another again. They were sitting on benches in the central roofed-over area between the sleeping huts and the resident Bantu-speakers were serving food and drink.

It was not difficult to imagine that this scene could have been enacted in similar fashion hundreds of, or even a thousand, years ago:a symbiotic relationship between subsis-tence-farmers and hunter-gatherers. It would not be difficult to compare this situation with one further south of here where commercial farmers were employing San to work on their farms. But the communication in this latter example did not work as well as I had wit-nessed along the Kavango. It was more a situation of the commercial farmers turning into prosecutors when the San wanted to leave after the rainy season.

DIKUNDU

I had another encounter with a San group at the third and last site I was working on, in the east of the Kavango territory, close to the border of the Caprivi. An informant from the nearby mission station had shown me to the site at Dikundu. Having found two sites with pottery, the one at Kapako and the other at Vungu Vungu, I had been looking for evidence of metalworking.

I was taken to a place in the savannah about thirty kilometres from the river. The very flat, stoneless area looked frighteningly uniform to me. I was amazed when my guide suddenly made me stop the car, got out and walked in a straight line to a certain spot, where he picked up a few pieces of slag. It seemed the most unlikely place for a furnace but the traces of slag were undeniable.

We slaved away clearing a heavy concentration of slag from vegetation and from the fine white Kalahari sand that covered the surface of the ground in an even layer. After three days of brushing and carting away bucket after bucket of fine sand, I decided that this could not have been the furnace but might have been a foundry where metal was heated a second time before it was forged into shape for tools or weapons. Consequently, I wanted to suggest that we explore the area in this vicinity more closely.

Once again I felt utterly crippled by not being able to speak the local language fluently. Back at the mission station where we were staying for the time being, I mentioned this to the priest, who was a friend of mine. He, fluent in the language, called in two old men and the most fascinating stories emerged. This would have been another golden opportunity for collecting oral tradition. First of all, they pointed out that the place where we had been working was indeed not the location of the furnace but the place where they were literally 'working' the metal. One man said that his grandfather had worked at the site. A few miles away from the place where we had found the slag, was an omuramba - a depression where water would collect during the rainy season. With enough rain omurambas would overflow and could join up to form a river. The old men were saying that the place where the metal had been smelted would be marked by red sand. It was on the edge of the omuramba close to where we had been working.

When we asked about the significance of the red sand they looked at us as though our ignorance was more than they could bear. Where did we think they would get the metal from that they were smelting? From the red sand, of course.

Now we heard the story of how the very first men had come to this area to show the local people how to smelt metal. They had come from the east and had brought five iron hoes and some other tools with them, as a gift for the local Mbukushu chief. In a message which they also had brought, their chief had asked whether there was any iron stone in this land. The Mbukushu chief told them about the red sand in the omuramba southwest from Dikundu.

The Chief said that the sand was as red as blood, and if the visitors would show the Hambukushu how to work with this sand, then they could come and make their tools here. So the visitors promised to show the Mbukushu how to use the red sand and for every tool or hoe that they made they promised to leave one with their host. They left very early the following day with empty bags and returned to Dikundu three days later with bags filled with the red sand. Every man had his own little pile of sand but they all worked around the same fire.

I had the red sand analysed and was amazed to learn that it contained 39% of pure ferrum - iron ore. I could not wait to go back to Dikundu and find the smelting site. We took the same road that led past the foundry site and came to the edge of the omuramba. The vegetation here was very dense but we soon found some slag. At the end of the first morning I had isolated a mound of slag and coal, which, I presumed was covering the furnace. Strangely enough I did not find the multitude of clay tuyères I would have expected. When I asked about tuyères I was told that here one used a part of the anthill. I did not quite understand this and asked for a demonstration. The following day a trumpet shaped tuyère was brought to me and I was taken to the anthill, where it was said to have been made. Apparently it was simply a bit of clay chopped out of the base of the anthill, which was then shaped and had a hole bored through it.

We pitched our camp under the canopy of trees that formed a little forest on the edge of the omuramba. I was nervous because time had as usual just flown past and we were really too far into the hot season to be safe from rain, mosquitoes and excessive heat. Had this been yet another tactic of my Museum Director to get at me, I was wondering? Our departure from Windhoek had been delayed for weeks because of special permission, which, he claimed, would have to be obtained from Pretoria for mileage that had exceeded the annual quota he had requested for my fieldwork. There had been arguments about my safety: A woman going 'alone' – with Mr Brits, a white man and Max, a Tswana man. It provoked me because I felt that it was insincere and only paid tribute to the accepted image of the incapable woman. After all I had been reluctant to take on the assignment in the first place for security reasons. By now I had invested time and energy and was keen to complete what I had started.

I was here and determined to finish my work at this site before leaving. I would just have to be on my guard against snakes and mosquitoes and see that I took enough salt to counter heat exhaustion and pray that the rains would not turn all the roads to mud before we left. With these thoughts in mind I was arranging my things in my tent that had been set up a short distance from the fireplace, the vehicle and the place where the men were sleeping. I was putting up my camping table and chair where it would be cooler, in front of the tent rather than inside. As I was doing this, I suddenly had the feeling of being watched. I turned around and gave a start when I saw a whole row of small people standing and looking at me. I had not heard a sound as they approached. Within a split second I gained control of myself and smiled, to have their faces light up in smiles in return.

"Mire", I said, which was a Nama greeting and I hoped they would understand it. There was some talking, but I could not identify the customary reply, which I would have expected. I wondered what to do next. I did not want them to go away so I called Max, who knew one of the San languages. He came over from where he and Brits were setting up a general dining-kitchen and living area next to the truck. He greeted them and I was relieved to find that he could obviously communicate with them.

He explained that a Hambukushu man who was living in a village not far from where we were camped had already told him that the San group had arrived a few weeks ago and were encamped on the other side of the omuramba. The Hambukushu man had wanted to know whether we would be employing people to help with our work. Possibly this was a kind of application for work.

The contingent that had come to my tent wanted me to come over to their camp. I felt terribly flattered and without much further ado I followed the single file as they were headed back across the omuramba. There was some chattering and laughing amongst my leaders, mostly young women and girls with three little boys aged perhaps five to eight. I had not the faintest idea what I was in for. Luckily I had grabbed my sling bag as I left my tent. At least I had some cigarettes and sweets in there, two commodities I had found to be useful on occasions of this sort.

When we reached the other side of the omuramba I noticed that there was another path, branching off from our path, which led to the water hole. I had not been there and made a mental note of it because I was looking forward to a refreshing wash that evening. Indeed, I thanked my lucky stars for once again being so fortunate as to have an abundant water supply near my camp. The path we followed curved into the bush that was high enough to conceal us walking upright. I could hear some chickens cackling in the distance and also thought I had heard goats. A little further along we passed an enclosure made from chopped-off bushes where the goats were herded together for the night. Rather suddenly we came upon a fairly large clearing in the bush. On the edge of it, about half a dozen small wide mouthed grass huts were arranged. A large tree stood a little off-centre in the crescent shaped clearing in front of the huts. A few men were lounging on skin karosses (blankets made of tanned skins) talking and smoking. One of them was cracking nuts on a dimpled stone. Another one was making link shafts for his arrows. I would have liked to walk over to the men to have a closer look at what they were doing, but an awareness of a general rule that women should stay with women made me follow my female companions to one of the far huts where some older women were sitting. I felt terribly large as I approached them, and simply decided to go down on my knees and squat like them, hoping that it would somehow decrease the social distance between us. Some excited calling and running to the next hut broke a slightly awkward silence, which might have arisen because, again, my Nama greeting had not been understood. I was trying to work out what was going on and could not help laughing when two chairs were brought: one for me, and one for my bag! I sat down on the chair and felt almost as though I was using furniture from a doll's house. I tried to gesture and make some noises that were meant as 'thank you'.

I joined in the general atmosphere of excited laughing and talking by also talking some clicklish language although I knew that no one understood what I said. But I had previously found that simply giving the impression of talking somehow helped the atmosphere and put people at ease. They talked a lot. I looked around, pointed at things that caught my interest, nodded and mimicked. One of the old women called a child, told her something and pulled a pipe out of a skin bag that was lying close to her. The child had gone to fetch some embers with which to light the pipe. The old lady took a few puffs and then handed the pipe on to the next woman. As a rule, I did not smoke other than puff on a cigarette every now and then. This was a pipe and I had no idea what was being used for tobacco. The next woman also took a few puffs and handed the pipe on. Intuitively I took out a cigarette and lit it up, took a few puffs and handed it to the woman next to me in the direction in which the pipe was approaching. My cigarette was greeted with smiles and obvious approval, and miraculously, the pipe disappeared. I lit up another cigarette!

The chatter in our group was calming down a bit and a few children left and went to another hut. Two of the older girls also got up to join a group of four or five young women on the other side of the central tree. They were sitting down close to one another and started to clap their hands ever so softly. I was delighted, particularly when I realised that they were also going to sing. At first it was very faint and had a high pitch, which then developed into a rhythmic, melodious chant. Painfully aware of my complete ignorance of any musicology, I nevertheless enjoyed what to me was an utterly sweet and pure sound. Just as I was wishing that I could get a little closer to the singers but was reluctant to leave my hostesses lest I should appear rude, a young man and a woman came up to me, or rather up to my chairs, and indicated that they wanted to move them. I followed them to where they resettled me on the far side of the singing group, opposite from where the men were sitting, underneath the trees. The clapping of hands and the singing were quite clear now. Two men then got up and without moving their feet, swayed to the music. Very slowly they were starting to shuffle in the direction of the women. Moving their feet next to each other in tiny steps they created two parallel lines of tracks. When they reached the singers they started to encircle them. I was enthralled. Although I knew that I would regret it later I was almost glad not to have my cameras with me so that I could concentrate solely on what was going on around me.

More men joined the circle and some of them also joined in the singing. After a while the singing ebbed away and the dancing stopped. One of the girls left the group but two others joined it. Then one of the men got up and chanted a tune. The women emulated him and a new dance was started. Two little toddlers were starting to move to the music as well and one of the men picked up one little boy and danced with him. When he put him down to dance with the other men around the women, the little child ran away crying. Just as casually as the dancing had started about an hour before, it now stopped. I took some of the sweets from my bag and gave them to the old lady who had started up the pipe. I tried to say goodbye as competently as I could and amidst smiles and general goodwill - or so I perceived - I started my way back to our camp.

Max and Brits were coming from the direction of the waterhole, laughing and chatting away, obviously refreshed by the 'bath' that - I presumed - they had taken. This was a good time for me to go and have that many splendoured thing - a wash. I went to collect my bag, towel and a change of clothes. Even the moon was in our favour being just in that phase when it rose almost as the sun set, providing a continuous, soft light. The air was mild with hardly a breath stirring. There was a wind pump over the water hole in the small clearing. The water flowed through a pipe to a round reservoir about two metres high. The reservoir was standing inside a round drinking trough, almost like a cup on a saucer. The water spilled over the edge of the reservoir into the drinking trough. The rim or edge of this trough was some 50 centimetres from the ground and a handy place for soap, washcloth and other odds and ends. I knelt and felt the lovely wetness on the skin of my hands and arms. The water was clean and I was contemplating just getting into the trough, boots and all, so to speak. It would spill the water, but that was all right, since in any case I was going to try and drain the soapy water off when I had finished. As so often in a camp situation I savoured the scent of my soap and consciously indulged in the refreshment provided by the combination of soap and that superb substance called water. Should I worry about possible passers-by or onlookers, I wondered, checking the dense wall of bush surrounding the little clearing with the wind pump, the water reservoir and me. Max and Mr Brits were over at the camp and not likely to come back here. The San were quite a distance away and it was pretty late to come and water the goats. So I decided to throw care to the wind and took off my warm, dusty clothing, feeling as though my whole body was taking a deep breath. I splashed water all over myself and then started on a thorough cleansing project. Suddenly some movement or noise startled me. I jerked to look around and must have gasped as I did so. A San man stepped into the clearing and as I gasped he started, ducked and looked around with a taut expression as if he had suddenly been warned of some danger. What on earth was I to do? I thought to myself. Obviously not seeing anything that he considered dangerous, he relaxed and straightened out and walked more or less straight towards me in the most natural way. It would have been utterly ridiculous to scream or try to cover up my nakedness with face cloth or soap - my towel was not within reach.

So I just knelt there, more or less stunned, I suppose, and watched the young man as he filled his gourd with water from the tap next to me and looked around once or twice as though he wanted to make quite sure that there was not anything to be worried about. I almost felt as though I should explain why I had got a bit of a fright but he would not have understood it. When his gourd was full, he knelt down to drink from the tap himself, and then, with a friendly nod in my direction, left just as quietly as he had come. After a minute or so I collapsed with a chuckle. His behaviour had been so completely natural that I looked down at myself to check whether I really had no clothes on and then continued with my washing ritual.

No more than fifteen minutes had passed when I heard voices and laughter.
What next? By now I was in clean clothes and was busy dressing a small cut on my finger when a group of about six women and children emerged from the bush. They had also come to fetch water and positioned themselves in half-moon formation around me, obviously fascinated by the many little jars and bottles that we consider necessary for our health and well-being. A little girl closest to the soap dish ventured a step in that direction and touched the soap with her pointed finger, pulled back quickly and smelt it. I took the cake of soap and demonstrated washing my hands, being watched closely. I then offered the soap to one of the young women who took it reluctantly but then stepped up to the trough and started to wash her hands and arms very thoroughly. The soap was handed on and everyone followed suit. Another event, which topped even this one in terms of the interest it evoked, happened a few days later when I shampooed my hair. The soft white suds had everyone touching and exclaiming in wonder.

Three of the men had enrolled at the dig and with two Hambukushu men from the nearby village, I once more had a willing team of local helpers. One of the San who understood some Afrikaans was, to me, the best example of an individual capable of adaptation that I had ever come across. He had a tattoo on his arm and when I asked about it, he told me that he had been working in the gold mines in Johannesburg. It was hard to have been living in the 'kampong' (compound) for three years, he assured me. He had also worked on a farm near Grootfontein. But he always came back to his group. His name was !Goma (with an initial click) and he would come to work in an overall which he never took off. The other two men came to work in tattered army jackets and the remains of dustcoats. But these they would take off and hang them in a tree when they started working, to be put on again when they went home.

We had cleared an area of 100 square metres and were brushing away white sand from traces of slag and charcoal. We found several semi-consolidated patches of very red sand, just as the two old men had predicted. A heavy concentration of slag, which had been dissected, did not yield any indication of a furnace structure. I was at a loss. A layer of charcoal with metal impurities was embedded in the white sand covering the area. This track petered out towards the edges of the grid we had cleared. On one side of it there was a termite mound about 1metre high, partly overgrown and seemingly no longer inhabited.

These termite workings or anthills were common in the area. I had quite carefully looked at those that I passed in short daily walks to see whether there was any striking difference between the one in our grid and the others in the vicinity. Subconsciously, I had probably contemplated the possibility of its significance right from the start, but that suspicion had not crystallised into a conscious investigation.

With no other alternative I followed the traces of slag that led to the base of the termite hill. Our base line extended just beyond the foot of the clay mound. Trying to scrape this red clay matrix with trowels was like trying to scrape away concrete.

Scraping the clay of the anthill was like trying to excavate in concrete (author and Max)

Our progress was excruciatingly slow and the trowels were wearing down quickly. I had visions of a report describing the exposure of natural termite workings, as we would break through the passages which were characteristically illustrated in section drawings of termite hills. When a passage seemed to be leading upward I imagined it to be part of a chimney. When the passage ran horizontally I wondered whether it might be a hole for a tuyère. But time after time it was just another ant path that curved into the subterranean part of the hill. One big duct leading down into the earth was so deep that we could not even reach the bottom with a stick two metres long. It very conveniently served the purpose of disposing of the clayey material we had loosened in the course of this unusual way of excavating. We simply swept the loosened debris down into this hole instead of lugging away heavy buckets. One day I got so frustrated with the uncertainty of picking through this anthill that I went and opened up another ant hill that had obviously not been disturbed by human hand. I had a good look at the pattern of the ducts there.

We had come across so many of them in our excavation. But I was puzzled when we came across what looked like two broad parallel lines approaching the vertical body of the antheap. Apparently they originated at the point where the upright wall of the anthill formed an angle to the base on the ground. There was coal and slag in between these two light-yellow seams. They had a lighter colour than the material that coated them.

It was terribly hot and everyone was working quietly. I decided to take a photograph of the extraordinary pattern that was appearing and which seemed to lead into the anthill. We had left one big bush standing near the centre of the area we had cleared of vegetation. In the shade of this bush I kept my camera bag and a tin trunk with tools and equipment, which would get so hot in the sun that I could not touch them. I was no more than three paces away from my bag when something moved in the bush. A black line shot up through the leaves. I uttered a piercing scream and dashed away with the black line at my heels. Although it took no more than a few seconds it felt as if I was running and jumping forever, a long black snake behind me. At the same time I felt objects flying through the air and when I stopped to look, all the workers were hurling whatever they could lay hands on at the snake and diverting its course. I was terrified that the serpent might dive into one of the big ducts and disappear into the termite hill. Who would want to continue working there? But I could not put all that into one big scream. My other thought was that it might be a harmless snake and should not be killed.

At the same time I was glad of my inborn fear of reptiles because this one certainly did not appear to be timid or wanting to get away. I tried to work out whether I was just imagining it or whether it had really come after me. If it had, one of the 'missiles' must have hit it very soon because otherwise it would surely have caught up with me. It was by now badly injured and one of the workers went up to it and hit it on the head with a shovel. It was a very long black serpent. I did not know snakes well enough to be able to identify it. The crew was clicking away excitedly. Mr Brits was examining the bright yellow eyes in the small diamond shaped head and Max was shaking his head and saying 'atatitata' which is like saying 'good grief'. !Goma came up to me and pointed at the sun where it was standing almost exactly overhead, saying:
"Missie sien die son daar? Die slang byt Missie nou — as die son, hy daar (and he pointed to just above the horizon in the west) die missie hy dood." (Madam sees the sun there? The snake bites Madam now - when the sun is there (pointing) - the madam is dead)
"Do you think it's a poisonous snake?" I asked Mr Brits.
"It's a black mamba," he said as a matter of fact.
"Really," I said incredulously, "surely they must be bigger than that, I mean fatter?"
"Hy baie-baie giftig" (he is very very poisonous) !Goma was assuring me.
I asked Max to get me my camera and took a number of photographs. We measured it: 2,18 metres.

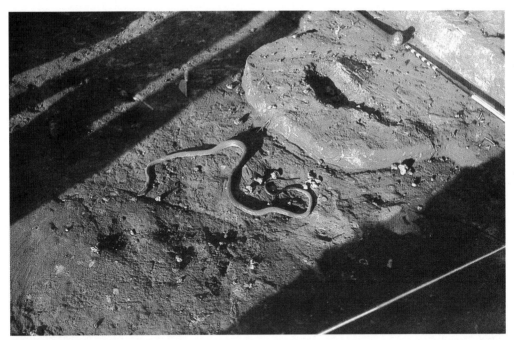

The serpent

!Goma and his colleague then took it and skinned it. One of them wound some string-like organ onto the end of a stick and said that it was poison he was going to use on his arrows. Or that is what I understood.

When we heard a car that afternoon and saw that it was not the army truck that came by almost every day, but visitors from the mission station, I was pleased and cancelled work for the day. The news they brought was not at all good. There was considerable unrest along the border on account of guerrilla activities and they wanted me to come and spend the night at the mission station. I thought of the horrible road and all the fuss, although that, of course, seemed much greater than it was in reality due to my state of utter exhaustion. I had also developed an open sore on my leg, probably a mosquito bite that had become infected. I felt I should just try and finish as quickly as possible and then leave for good. Going back and forth to the station would delay my stay by at least a day. I explained this to the lay priest and also said that, as on all previous visits, I had informed the police and the army of my whereabouts and that they had assured me of their care and that they would warn me in the event of any danger. It only struck me then that the army car, which had come by so often might, in fact, have been a sort of check on whether I was all right, although they had never said so. I must admit that I had neither been too friendly nor had I offered any hospitality when they had come by. I generally resented interruptions in my work.

The lay priest was not very happy with my decision and I was not at all sure whether I was doing the right thing either. Probably I was simply afraid that if I went to the mission station I might not return to the site ever again.

It seemed to get hotter by the hour and the sores on my leg were festering. We had made good progress with the exposure of the furnace, which, after all, turned out to be located

The clay furnace at Dikundu was located in the anthill

Dancing and singing in the moon light.....

in the anthill. It had been shaped like a boot. The shoe part was where the bellows were situated to blow air into the fire and this was the part indicated by the two parallel lines. We had dissected the furnace and had drawn a section and a plan. This gave a good idea of what it must have looked like when in action. It did not look strikingly different from clay furnaces I had seen in Malawi as well as in illustrations. I was satisfied that this excavation would be useful documentation of metal smelting in a clay furnace, probably with clay tuyères. It would clearly contrast with the smelting of metal involving stone tuyères and no clay. As we were photographing and plotting I calculated how many more hours we would have to spend at Dikundu. My estimate was that we could leave the following day but I did not want to announce this until I was sure.

That evening I was once more invited to go and visit my new San friends. My leg was throbbing and I had a splitting headache, but I knew that invitations like this would not come my way very often. I took a couple of aspirin, cleaned the wound as best I could by soaking it in warm soapy water, dressed it and went off across the omuramba and along the little path, which I knew quite well by now. I had been over to the little village on a few occasions in the meantime and had also taken some photographs but this was the first time that I would be going after dark.

The moon came up later and when it did appear, it looked like a huge slightly dented, pale yellow balloon. Again there was dancing and singing and as the moon came up it gave the whole scene the most intriguing lighting effect. The group of women who were singing and clapping were sitting on the edge of the shadow cast by the canopy of the large tree that was standing in the central area in front of the huts. When men, dancing around them in a circle, entered the shadow they could no longer be seen, but they would reappear as they emerged from the shadow coming around on the other side of the circle. As before, every new dance was opened by one of the men chanting a new tune, which was then taken up by the singers. After they had swayed to the music for a few minutes, the man who had suggested the new song started to move forward and gradually others would join him, until there was a full circle of dancers moving around the group of singers sitting on the ground. The light was not very good and I could not distinguish individual dancers. However, !Goma was easily recognizable because he was wearing his overall. This garb did look a bit out of place amongst the other dancers who wore G-string type loincloths that came between the legs and had two flaps at the back reminiscent of large ears or tails. Some of them had rattles attached to their knees or ankles. Perhaps !Goma did not feel comfortable in his big heavy overall because I noticed how he started to withdraw one arm from a sleeve as he entered the shadow of the tree and could no longer be seen. When he came into the light again he was minus overall and in the same costume as his fellow dancers.

I ran a temperature that night. It was unbearably hot and the throbbing pain had moved to my groin. I had to leave the next day. The thing I dreaded most were the arguments that inevitably arose, when after weeks of toil in making a hole, I requested the workers to fill it in again before I left. It was a problem that I was incapable of solving. I had tried a number of different approaches, all of which had failed. When I told one of them that the hole we were going to dig would have to be filled in again, they practically refused to work, and when they did, it was impossible to get them to go carefully. Arguments about the danger of an unguarded, steep hole were countered by a host of practical alternatives for filling in the hole, such as 'but we will tell everybody about it' to suggesting that it would be easier to chop down a few bushes and place them around the hole. At one point it got so bad that I myself no longer knew whether I cared about that damn hole being filled in or not!

The saddest thing of all was that what had usually been a very pleasant working relationship often ended on a sort of bitter note because of that filling-in part. I think many of the workers thought somehow I had played the fool with them. Paying out extra money as a reward for the hard job of filling in at the end often appeared to be taken as an insult added to injury. And so, I am afraid, we also left Dikundu with slightly mixed feelings. Dr Maria Fisch at the mission station attended to my leg and recommended that I get to Windhoek as soon as possible because these bush sores left ugly scars when they were not properly taken care of.

The dates for the excavations along the Kavango were very interesting. It almost looked as though I had started with the earliest site and had then gradually worked my way forwards through time. Deep down in the test pit at Kapako we had found pottery that dated back to 850 A.D. It did not in any way resemble present day ware in use by the local population. Yet it resembled Bantu pottery from other parts of southern Africa. The Vungu Vungu site, where the first Sambiu Chieftainess was said to have erected her kraal when her tribe first arrived in this area, had a date of 1650 A.D. This came closer to the idea of the history of the area. Also the pottery from Vungu Vungu had affinities with present day pottery that made it plausible that the two were related. The most recent date was derived from a charcoal sample from the furnace site at Dikundu, placing it to the beginning of the twentieth century. Probably the smelter we had excavated was the one which the two old informants at the mission station had been talking about.

If there was no break in the sequence of occupation along the Kavango from 850 A.D. onwards then that would mean that a well-developed traditional method of potmaking and metalworking had been in practice here throughout that time. Spherical pots with rounded bases would have been in use and metal would have been smelted in anthills or clay furnaces. Trumpet-shaped clay tuyères had been brought from the area east of the Kavango. How does this picture along the northern border of Namibia relate to the one further south, in the central and southern parts of the territory? Here bag-shaped pots with pointed bases and very little decoration appear to have been contemporary with a metal working technique that made no use of clay, either for tuyères or furnaces. Sheep, which featured in the southern areas, have rarely been documented along the Kavango. Evidence of cattle on the other hand, has been found in both areas. The samples that were dated from the Rehoboth copper working site also go back to the mid-seventeenth century. That would mean that two different traditions were coexisting in SWA/Namibia three to four hundred years ago. Perhaps longer?

A few months after the work at Dikundu I met a young man who had been stationed up at the Kavango as part of the police force. We exchanged notes on our experiences up there. Suddenly he looked bewildered and exclaimed:
"You were camped at Dikundu?"
"Yes, why?"
"Do you know that you nearly caused a riot?" It was my turn to look bewildered.
"You see, we were told that a woman doing some work - that no one was able to explain - was going to be camped at Dikundu. We were told that she had been assured of our

protection and guards had been posted at strategic positions within a few miles of her camp. Apart from that a patrol car went by to see whether she was all right at least once a day. The reason for all this precaution was that it was feared that 'terrorists' (or freedom fighters), if they were to find out about a camp like that with a good store of food and other useful provisions might want to raid it. Everything was O.K. until they had that incident a few miles beyond Andara Mission Station."

"Was that when two of the boats were sunk and a policeman killed?" I interrupted.

"Yes. There was great excitement and for some reason that day no one drove by your camp to check whether you were all right - and that must have been the day you left. You didn't tell anyone you were going to leave that day, did you?" He asked.

"No. I wasn't certain I was actually going to leave that day until practically that morning. Now that you mention it, I must admit that I neglected to inform the police or army when I left because I felt pretty grim and just wanted to get home."

"Well, when we went to see you the next morning we found your camp deserted, and tracks of shoes that were only worn by a certain group of 'guerrillas' were all over the area. When we drove on we fell into a car trap - you know these ambushes they make, by digging a deep hole across the tracks and then covering them up with bush and sand. Well, we practically disappeared into one of those and I thought it would be tickets because the usual thing is that they lie in ambush and then just descend on you when you are stuck in the hole and you don't really have a chance."

I gasped.

"And what happened?" I asked, telling myself that whatever had happened he must have got away, because he was sitting and telling me this.

"We also don't know what happened, but as there was no-one lying in ambush; they must have changed their plans for some unknown reason. I tell you we were in a flat panic about you because, if something had happened to you, we would not only have been blamed for that but also for letting a golden opportunity pass by of catching them. After all, we were supposed to be prepared for them to raid your camp."

Hell. I had sometimes thought about what I would do if I were actually confronted by freedom fighters. My friend, Pauline Marè, had sworn that I would have talked them into digging for me before they knew what had hit them. I must admit, my thoughts had run along those lines.

The young policeman was looking at me and shaking his head:

"You know, I often wondered about that woman. I thought she must be stone mad. I thought that perhaps she was a fanatic who was trying to punish herself for something by working up there. I just could not imagine someone going and working there out of his or her own free will. I never expected to meet her."

In Namibia such coincidences are not uncommon. People knew one another and knew about one another. Gossip was rife and it was difficult to be anonymous. The architects of Apartheid had structured our numerically small, heterogeneous society quite rigidly. Could Apartheid be enforced less rigorously here than in South Africa, because everyone knew everyone else? The Apartheid philosophy assumed that the most critical boundary markers of the different groups, as they were identified by Apartheid's architects, would always coincide. In other words, people with a certain appearance would speak the same language, share the same religion and have similar tastes and priorities. Consequently the term 'culture' embraced all these issues and was definitive and determined by the concept of race. No effort was spared to ensure endogamy - marriage within the cultural group. The Mixed Marriages Act – a law forbidding marriages across the colour line - went so far as to empower the police to inspect the parking places where lovers would go at night and to arrest those who loved someone of a different skin colour. The nickname of one policeman was Bumpercollin because he would check whether the bumpers of the parked cars were moving rhythmically. In such cases he would take pleasure in interrupting the coitus by law!

In spite of such draconian measures people still fell in love with one another, made love and had children who automatically belonged to more than one group on the basis of the artificial criteria that were supposed to distinguish the groups from one another. Many couples immigrated to other countries. Others tried to dodge the law in devious ways. Many love affairs and relationships ended tragically because partners were forcibly separated.

But the offspring was there and had to be sorted out somehow. During a census held in the eighties, citizens were requested to indicate which cultural or racial group they belonged to. They had 68 categories to choose from. People like me who failed to identify with any one of these 68 groups on account of my German-Jewish background, non-practising, christened Roman Catholic, had the option of putting their cross with group No. 69: entitled OTHER. Possibly this unacceptable identification contributed to my status as 'security risk' and consequently as persona-non-grata. My having studied in the U.S.A. - as a single woman – a woman alone - and in having gone as far as to marry an American, compounded the problem.

At that time the notion of racist or rightwing Americans had not yet taken root in South Africa. Wade, as a social anthropologist, did nothing to promote the image of the American who was in favour of separate development. Not surprisingly, our efforts at getting Wade employment in Namibia failed. This put a great strain on our relationship because I was reluctant to emigrate to the United States. My reluctance increased when an officer of the Special Branch (of the South African Police) talked to me 'as a friend' one day. His advice was that I leave the country because people like me only made things more difficult for the government.

Wade had to go back to the States to complete the work on his doctoral thesis. He had also been offered a position at the University of California, San Diego. I followed him a year later in 1971 to prepare the final draft of my dissertation. This time there was no Dr Steyn to facilitate my career as an archaeologist in Namibia. On the contrary, the conflicts of interest at the State Museum had taken on new proportions. This accelerated my resignation together with that of all the other professional staff who had worked there under Dr Steyn. An appeal to investigate matters at the museum resulted in a letter from a Member of Parliament in South Africa. He explained that a political appointment at the museum was more important at that point in time than any other consideration and that no further insubordination by staff would be tolerated.

In 1972 Wade and I managed to secure positions - albeit temporary ones - at South African universities. Wade had been granted leave to teach at Wits and at U.C.T. and I had a one-year appointment at The University of the Western Cape. I, too, had been awarded my doctoral degree. Our aim was to organise possibilities for both of us to work in Namibia. The only opportunity of working in Namibia which presented itself to me was in the form of a research project to be carried out at the Namib Desert Research Station, Gobabeb. I clung to that and Wade returned to his position at the University of California in San Diego. The marriage did not survive another long separation.

CHAPTER 7

THE UNIVERSITY OF THE WESTERN CAPE

"Is there anyone in this class who comes from South West Africa - or has at least been there?" I asked by way of introducing myself to the Anthropology class of 1972 at the University of the Western Cape – the university for so-called 'coloured' people of mixed descent. A few hands went up slowly. I was pleased to know the family of one of the students: Leslie Maasdorp. His uncle had shown me to the metal working site on the outskirts of Rehoboth and his cousin, Raymond, had helped with the excavation at the Drierivier copper-smelting site. Marylin Hoff came from Windhoek and Browne Neels hailed from Aroab, a village in the very rural, far south of the country. Altogether there were about thirty students in the class.

The first lectures of the course dealt with the theory of evolution and Physical Anthropology. The students were submissive and carefully took notes without asking any question or making any comments. In the South Africa of the time that was the kind of behaviour expected of good students at school, as well as at university. The accepted way of dealing with doubts about evolution from a religious point of view was to point out that it was - only - a *theory*.

In my lectures on Social Anthropology I presented information on various kinds of societies, which the creature called *Homo sapiens sapiens* had developed over the millennia. The South African society was compared to other societies worldwide. In particular, I chose the Indian caste society and the American class society for in-depth study. Hunter-gatherer societies and nomadic herder societies were discussed. Peasants worldwide were shown to share a number of characteristics, such as a conservative attitude to any kind of social change. Although class attendance was good, students made no attempt to apply the principles under discussion to their own society. I was longing for some challenge or criticism. Was this some kind of rejection? I asked myself. But these young men and women looked too shy, too uncertain to be capable of such a sophisticated way of communicating their disapproval.

I invited the Namibian students to my home and took them on an excursion around the beautiful Cape Peninsula. They had scarcely been beyond the borders of the university campus on the Cape Flats, that sandy stretch of land between the Cape Peninsula and the rest of the continent. I was very pleased when they accepted the invitation but even in the private, informal setting the atmosphere was not relaxed. I had borrowed my father's minibus and we spent most of the time in the car. That was the best way of avoiding the uncomfortable feeling of being conspicuous as a so-called 'white' person in the company of so-called 'non-whites'. Conversely there was a similar feeling of uneasiness. How would one explain a white woman being the driver for non-whites? In a battered old VW combi? Had we known each other a bit better it might have been possible to discuss these things openly, but we were all victims of that devastatingly effective, debilitating system called Apartheid.

Occasionally students would ask to see me after class and I gladly met them in my office, which I was sharing with a man of the cloth. Dominee Smit belonged to the Dutch Reformed Church, which was powering the South African theocracy. The Apartheid policy was based on passages from the Bible that assigned the bearers of water and the cutters of wood to their own special place. Contrary to my expectation we got on very well. He was an academic and approached me in a respectful and polite way. Inevitably the theory of evolution was up for discussion and I was impressed by Dominee Smit's reaction.

When students posed the ever-popular question: " How do the theory of evolution and the Bible relate to one another?" I invited the Dominee to join the discussion. The way he handled the issue has been an example I have been following ever since.
"A basic question," he said, "is whether you take the Bible literally or figuratively. If we can agree that the Bible speaks figuratively everything falls into place. The Bible states that God created heaven and earth, light and darkness, the waters of the sea, the dry land and all living creatures in the water and on the land before God on the sixth day created the human being. If you compare these biblical statements with the discoveries reported by scientists it is amazing how accurately scientific research reflects the report of God's work given in the Bible.

If we can agree that the first Day mentioned in the Bible was not equivalent to our day of 24 clock hours, then the First Day could relate to a time period, figuratively speaking. It may have lasted a few million years. Accordingly, scientific research confirms *how* the waters of the sea and the earth's crust came to be. The discovery of fossils in geological layers reflects the same order in which the appearance of life is described in the Bible; that is that the creatures in the seas preceded life on dry land. Only on the sixth day, the Bible states, did God create the human being. Compare that with the palaeontological evidence of plants, animals, and finally *Homo sapiens* making their appearance as recently as fifty or a hundred thousand years ago, well after the creatures of the sea and the land had been created. To me, as a devout Christian," he would say: "There is no conflict between what the Bible states and what science explains. Indeed, I find it marvelous how scientific research embellishes the amazing creation of God."

One day I was called into the office of a high ranking official in the university administration. A group of students in front of the Administration Building were milling around in a rather disorderly fashion. Some were holding placards. Others seemed to be arguing amongst themselves. There was coming and going. The atmosphere was tense. I was anxiously trying to smile at one or two faces I recognised, wondering whether it would make them uncomfortable to be greeted by a white person. What would happen if I joined them? Without even knowing what the demonstration was about, I could simply show solidarity.

A section of the Water Affairs trench showing layers of sand and layers of beach deposit (Photo: H.Scholz)

I picked up a stone. It was a smooth, well-rounded, water-worn cobble like those to be found along the seashore on the other side of the dune belt. I had not noticed any cobbles or pebbles in the walls of the trench where I had been walking. A few steps further along there were more stones of that kind. Then I picked up a fragment of oyster shell. I had also seen one of those before! It resembled oyster shells, many of them fully fossilised, which we had found at Meob Bay a few hundred kilometres south of where we were. Tony

Tankard, a South African marine biologist had identified my finds from there and according to him *Striostrea margaritacea* was a type of marine oyster, which lived in warm shallow water some two million years ago, I seemed to remember. My heartbeat accelerated. The wind was pelting us with small grains of sand and I slid back down into the trench.

"It looks like a whole layer with shells, cobbles and pebbles here, Beatrice," Mary was further along in the trench and was already taking photographs. A layer with an obviously different consistency from the sandy layers above and below it was stretching along the trench wall for as far as we could see from the limited angle we had inside the trench. Different kinds of shells, pebbles, cobbles and stones with holes as though drilled by worms were sticking out of the soil profile. Although we were utterly fascinated with what we had found we could not help but take note of the wind, which was now also blowing gusts of loose sand along inside the trench. We decided to call it a day.

We drove back to Swakopmund in high spirits because we had found '*something*'. Whom would we tell? My mother, of course, and her friend, Dr Weber, founder of the Swakopmund Museum. They would share our excitement, but who could tell us more than what we were telling ourselves at the moment? We had found shells and beach pebbles in the sand dunes! Tony Tankard was far away and I did not know him well enough to pick up the phone and tell him about this. That would have to wait until I had written up a report and had sent him carefully collected samples of our finds.

"We should try and call in a geologist," Mary said, as though she was reading my thoughts. "Perhaps Dr Scholz would be interested in looking at this," I wondered. He was a soil scientist and had recently published his dissertation on soils in the central Namib Desert. He had also visited the fossil site at Otjiseva where I had worked a few years before.

"Yes, why not. You have worked with him before and he probably knows more about soils in the Namib Desert than anyone else."

Remembering the work at Otjiseva I joked:

"Perhaps what we believe to be shell fragments will turn out to be porcelain…"

On the farm Otjiseva, some fifty kilometres north of Windhoek, on the edge of the escarpment, road workers had found fragments of what they thought were clay pots. On closer inspection these 'potsherds' had turned out to be fragments of a fossilised human skull. I had decided to do an excavation of the site in the hope of finding more parts of the skeleton. Apart from a single fossilised vertebra I could only document a layer of surface limestone, which made excavation all but impossible. The formation of limestone was interesting because it implied climatic change and scientists were working on methods of dating limestone.

The fossilised bones found at Otjiseva had been covered with a layer of hardened lime, which was dated to an age of ten thousand years. That was the only indication of age associated with those skeletal remains. Middle Stone Age artefacts, which were found in the vicinity of the fossil bone fragments, could not be linked directly to the skeleton. The stone tools could be at least thirty thousand years old, probably much older. In Malawi our finds of Middle Stone Age tools with the remains of an elephant had been estimated to be one hundred or even one hundred and fifty thousand years old. An analysis of the reconstructed skull from Otjiseva by Hertha de Villiers at the University of the Witwatersrand had indicated that the individual might have belonged to a physical type, which preceded the development of characteristics today displayed by the Khoe-San people in southern Africa.

But no date had yet been postulated for that specialised development. It could therefore be argued that the layer of limestone on the bones might have developed when there was a climatic change in these regions a long time after the person, whose fossilised remains had been found, had lived and died here. The fact that there was no datable collagen left in the bone could support the older age of the fossils. A variety of different local conditions could have influenced the disintegration of collagen. Once more I had been confronted with the possibility of being in touch with an ancestor of the human race.

The theme of climatic change was fascinating and I was delighted to have been given the task of documenting changes in our climate by finding associated datable archaeological material. I had only become aware of the scientifically documented worldwide phenomenon of climatic change as a graduate student. Before that time I had associated concepts such as the Ice Ages with fantastic jokes, which some crazy scientists had thought up. In more educated circles the European Ice Ages probably were known as examples of climatic change. But distinctions between the Günz, Mindel, Riss or Würm Alpine Ice Ages still fell within the realm of the esoteric. Among specialists in southern Africa, often self-taught, the assumption was made that climatic changes in Africa were contemporaneous with the Ice Ages in Europe, only a bit watered down: while there had been ice and snow in Europe there would have been cooler weather with more rain in Africa. Increasingly specialists from a wide range of fields were working on comparing the different kinds of data collected. I was overawed by theories and arguments in this universe of special knowledge and wondered whether I would be able to keep up with all the information that was forthcoming. I admired Mary who seemed to cope so well.
"Stick to carefully documenting your finds," Keith used to say when our discussions turned to complicated theories.
"If you observe accurately, and describe correctly what you are doing, then you have contributed valuable data which the armchair archaeologists can interpret or misinterpret as they like."

I was finding my niche as a dirt archaeologist. Ultimately I would have to link up with one or other grand scheme or I might even design my own, I thought. For the time being I had my hands full with organizing myself in the field. That implied prioritising because it was impossible to do everything. I was quickly discovering that fieldwork priorities were often influenced by pragmatic considerations. Fellow students of Dr Clark had often mused about what would have happened to our beloved Professor if he had not had his wife Betty making sure that he would take along that bottle of water, a sandwich or a first aid kit. There was consensus among us that he would have succumbed to starvation and exposure long before he became famous. A competent 'wife', it was generally agreed, was a precondition for becoming a good archaeologist. Is getting to become a good archaeologist my only aim in life? What was a good archaeologist and in whose eyes? Who do you want to think that you are a good archaeologist? I asked myself.

A few weeks after our discovery of sea shells in the Water Affairs trench Dr Scholz came to look at the site. He thought the layer with shells and water-worn cobbles might represent a buried beach or part of a river estuary dating back to times before the dune strip between Walvis Bay and Swakopmund had formed. The finds of warm-water oyster shells that had lived here approximately two million years ago supported this theory.

The Namib Desert Research Station was located on the northern bank of the oasis-like Kuiseb River, marking the boundary between the dune field and the plains Namib

With such questions at the back of my mind I started to establish myself at the Namib Desert Research Station, Gobabeb. Mary Seely showed me all the archaeologically interesting places known to her in the Namib Naukluft Park and soon more sites were

After the rains the Kuiseb River reminded me of paradise

The Kuiseb winding its way through the Damara system

added to the list as I started to move around on my own or in the company of fellow researchers on trips which they undertook to places which were not as yet known to me.

The Namib Desert Research Station was situated on the Kuiseb River's northern bank where three different natural zones were converging upon one another. The oasis-like riverbed clearly divided the huge sand-dune field of the central Namib from the gravel plains hemming the northern riverbank. The 100 millimetre isohyet, that line linking up places with similar rainfall, was considered to be a boundary between the very arid coastal part of the desert to the west and the pro-Namib further east reaching out towards the central highlands where rainfall was gradually increasing. Some features of the winter rainfall zone, that is rain during the winter months in the Cape, would occasionally occur as far north as the Kuiseb River.

The extensive catchment area of this river encompassed much of the Khomas Hochland. Travelling westward from Windhoek one crossed the Kuiseb and its tributaries winding their way through ranges of the Damara System forming the scenic Namib escarpment. The most impressive crossing occurred where the Kuiseb River entered its canyon, which snakes through steep mica schist cliffs up to Homeb, a Topnaar settlement upstream from Gobabeb.

At Homeb layers of ancient mud flank the mountainous canyon wall along the northern riverbank before it starts flattening out into the gravel plains. These massive layers of mud could only have been deposited in still water as might be found in a lake or vlei. We found the shells of small fresh water snails in these silt deposits and they were dated to an age of approximately 23 000 years by the radio carbon 14 method. These little old shells indicated a dry period when sand dunes blocked the surface flow of the Kuiseb River. The same thing was now happening at Sossus and Tsondab Vlei.

113

At Homeb layers of ancient silt flank the walls of the canyon (Photo C.K. Brain)

On the Kuiseb's southern bank the high sand dunes continued along the course of the river up to the ocean. Approximately 20 kilometres from the coast the (usually) dry river-bed spreads out in a way that makes it difficult to follow the main stream. A huge delta area consists of sandy hummocks often overgrown, and of smaller dunes bordering on

With Christian Dering, a student volunteer,I found tiny snail shells in the silt deposits at Homeb

densely vegetated stretches containing a variety of plant species. There are wet patches and pools of water some of which merge into extensive saltpans close to the shore. Shell middens like the ones we found at Meob Bay also dot this delta-like area.

Possible end point of the Kuiseb River (1974) disappearing in the dunes west of Rooibank

Similar distinctive landscapes along the Namibian coast occur roughly across from where riverbeds running from east to the west end in vleis or pans in the dunes. Only the two large rivers marking Namibia's northern and southern boundary, the Kunene River and Orange River are perennial. All the other rivers crossing the Namib Desert carry water into the Atlantic Ocean only seasonally or seep away into the dune sand before their surface flow can reach the sea. A careful look at the map of the area reveals an interesting pattern. Most noticeable are the inroads made into the sand-dune field by the Tsauchab River ending in Sossus Vlei, the Tsondab leading into Tsondab Vlei, the Tsams into Tsams Vlei and the Koichab into Koichab Pan. Driving along the eastern edge of the dune field between Swakopmund and Walvis Bay the same phenomenon can be observed on a small scale by unnamed little watercourses. The railway line marks the eastern edge of the narrow dune strip and crosses culverts bridging small drainages, which mark the phenomenon in that area. They end in tiny pans in the dunes where !nara bushes (*Acanthosicyos horridus*), the dollar bush (*Zygophyllum stapffii*) and tamariskia (*Tamarix*) grow.

On a satellite photograph of the southern Namib obvious irregularities are noticeable in the otherwise rhythmic pattern of the long north-south dune ranges in the sea of sand. These disconformities tell the history of river courses, which once upon a time carried surface water to the sea until their flow was blocked by sand dunes.

Conception Bay and Meob Bay are places where rivers used to flow into the sea. Nowadays a weak flow of fresh water continues to trickle down to the coast beneath the sand dunes

Sattelite photo of the Kuiseb River area (Photo: C.K. Brain)

and surfaces in the form of springs (Reutersbrunn, Fischersbrunn) or lagoons close to the coast. The time intervals at which the Kuiseb River and the Swakop river have been reaching the sea are growing longer and longer. They could well be representing a stage which the Tsauchab River and others underwent a long time ago.

The observations that had been made so far only allowed a rough reconstruction of ancient river valleys in the Namib Desert. The archaeological contribution to this entertaining story was the finding of stone tools in the dune field where human life today can only be sustained with modern technology: hi-tech transport, ice boxes and air conditioners. Whoever had produced the Early Stone Age artefacts we were finding along these ancient fossil riverbeds could not have survived under present conditions. These stone tools were made by the ancestors of the human race and resembled Early Stone Age tools found elsewhere which would have been made and used between one hundred and fifty thousand years and three million years ago.

The prehistoric horizon which I had visited at Mwanganda's site in Malawi had to be pushed back that much further. At that East African early Middle Stone Age site I had

An Early Stone Age hand-axe found west of Tsondab Vlei.

imagined the actors to be slightly different from us biologically modern human beings. I had thought of them as some or other type of *Homo erectus*. At Berg Aukas near Grootfontein a fossilised femur had been found in 1968 which, according to Phillip Tobias, was almost identical to the femur of a *Homo neanderthalensis* discovered at Spy in Belgium. The same early human species may have made the well-shaped hand axes and cleavers, which we found in the central Namib Desert.

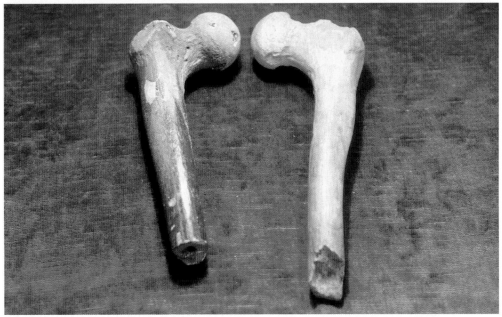

The Berg Aukas femur (slightly blackened) with a cast of the femur found at Spy in Belgium (Photo: C.K. Brain)

But we also found chopping tools or pebble choppers which had been made even longer ago than that. We were talking about the very first consciously made stone tools ever produced by members of our lineage. In South and East Africa such artefacts have been discovered in association with skeletal remains of early humans who pre-dated *Homo erectus* and *Homo Neanderthalensis* before *we* – the crowning glory of it all – *Homo sapiens*, arrived on this planet as recently as a few hundred thousand years ago.

Since the beginning of the 20th century palaeontologists and anthropologists have been finding remains of ever more 'missing links' in East and South Africa: the Australopithecines walking on two legs dated back three to four million years. Myra Shackley had found remains of an extinct elephant species (*Elephas reckii*), in the sand dunes south of the Kuiseb River. That was an indication of climatic conditions there during the Pleistocene which commenced some two million years ago.

The jaw bone of a likely predecessor of *Australopithecus* – that is *Otavipithecus namibiensis* – had been found in bone breccia in the Otavi mountains. Although the fossil femur of *Homo erectus* had been found in the same mountain, *Otavipithecus* lived approximately 10 - 12 million years earlier. That date was based on the identification of fossil rodent bones associated with *Otavipithecus.*

The right lower jaw of Otavipithecus namibiensis still partially impacted in the bone breccia from Berg Aukas – actual size ± 10 cm long

The evidence we were collecting was not only documenting past climatic changes, but was also highlighting that Namibia was occupying a corner if not more of the emerging cradle of humanity on this planet. Early Stone Age tools had also been found in other parts of the country and I was starting to believe that many more discoveries were simply waiting to be made. I remember a kind of fear of actually spelling out these ideas to myself. What is it that is so frightening? I asked myself. The answer was that I myself had difficulty believing it and coping with it.

ANCIENT TRACKS NEAR TSONDAB VLEI

On an expedition across the dune sea south of the Kuiseb River we noticed a light-coloured layer of dried mud eroding out of the red dune sand. On closer inspection it looked like the surface of a riverbed or vlei after the water had dried up and the well-known pattern of mud cracks had started to develop in the process. We were near Tsondab Vlei and were speculating about this having been an arm of the Tsondab River or an ancient part of the vlei at some point in the past.

Armed with my paint brush and trowel I swept away a bit of sand from where this horizontal layer was disappearing beneath the dune. There were some marks on the mudcracked surface: foot prints of birds! I wanted to go on sweeping away some more sand, but my learned colleagues were blowing the car's hooter – time to drive on. I noted the location of this spot as carefully as possible because I was determined to return to it for a closer look with no other item on the agenda than to find out whether more marks or finds might be buried beneath the dune sand.

I actually managed to persuade my friends Klaus Ahlert and Dr Hans Scholz to accompany me on this mission. When Pieter Mostert of the Department of Nature Conservation at Gobabeb heard about my plans he promised back-up if needed.

We picked our route across the sand-sea by driving on the well-compacted windward slopes of the dunes and by sliding down the loose slip faces when we had to change direction. There were no tracks or prominent features in this landscape and I was praying that my notes and my memory were going to lead me back to that strip of white clay that had been lacing the foot of one of the innumerable sand dunes that were stretching out as far as the eye could see. I felt a bit like a dog sniffing the air to catch a whiff of where 'my' tracks might be.... an archaeological dog whose sense of smell could transcend aeons of time…

By some miracle I suddenly recognised a slight depression from where a low sand terrace formed that edge on which that remarkable clay layer still was in position. Leaping out of the car I made a dash for my bird track and was beaming as I pointed it out to Klaus and Hans. Their faces expressed incredulity and pity.
"What would you like us to do?"
"Well," I was looking for something to say.
"I wanted to see whether there might be more tracks on this layer and…."
"More tracks of birds?" Klaus asked with a frown.
"Or perhaps other animals," I was trying to regain some lost ground,
"or even other things."
Hans, the geologist, pointed out that this layer might be extending for many metres underneath this sand dune.
"Although it is not one of the very high dunes," he offered lamely to make it sound less daunting, I suppose. But he had certainly taken the wind out of my sails.
"What on earth was I doing here?" it echoed through my mind.
In the meantime Klaus had fetched a hand broom and a brush from the car and was on his knees sweeping away some sand from the white clayey surface. The least I could do was to show solidarity with this gesture of loyalty. I followed suit and went to sweep up some red dune sand from the clay layer a few metres further along the foot of the dune. Hans took his geological hammer and said he was going to do some general reconnaissance in

119

the area.

"That's a good idea," I said trying to regain my composure while I was brushing the foot of a sand dune in the central Namib Desert west of Tsondab Vlei!

"Beatrice!" Klaus was calling,
"Come and have a look. Somehow the surface seems to be sloping down here."
Although I could not really see what he meant I encouraged him to follow that perceived trend to see whether it was continuing in the same direction or whether it would again be changing. I did, however, notice some beetle remains in the cracks of the dried mud fragments. I collected them for Sebastian Endroedy, an entymologist at the Transvaal Museum. He told me that those beetles were no longer found in the Namib dunes.

The hot air could be seen in little ripples just above the surface of the all-engulfing sheets of sand around us. In the distance Hans was the only other living feature moving in this environment. Walking back to my small corner of brushed sand I was fighting impulse and confusion. Klaus called again:
"Now it's bending upwards!"

Unreal. Now, I too, could see a definite impression or depression in the clayey surface like a large groove with a U-shaped section. Carefully removing the loose sand from the hard-ened matrix of dry mud, we found that the groove had two ends like a longish oval dish or bowl.
"Let us remove all the sand around the edges so that I can get a good picture of this strange feature here," I was saying as I was already starting to gently move the loose sand into the dustpan to then toss it away at arm's length.
"Here it's going down again!" Klaus almost shrieked.
He was right. There was another gentle downward bend in the mud-cracked surface less than a foot away from the edge of the 'groove' we were trying to clear.
Hans had come back from his reconnaissance.
"What are you doing here?" Mild surprise and curiosity in his voice.
"Look at this unnatural depression in the clay. Isn't that odd?" Without really expecting an answer I had recovered enough self-confidence to suggest him getting the other tools from the car and then helping us to remove more sand - gently.
He also brought back a very welcome thermos of cold water. I do not remember us taking any real break. We were brushing, sweeping, shoveling and blowing away sand from an amazing track of eleven, evenly spaced prints on what once must have been a malleable surface of moist clay. The weight of whatever had made the prints must have been greater than that of the bird which made only a very slight impression in the mud. But it could not have been too great or the mud would have cracked conspicuously.

Groping for an explanation of what may have caused these marks or prints, ideas ranged from the sublime to the ridiculous. Although we tried to imagine a plant or a natural physical phenomenon that could have brought about such a set of tracks, we could not come up with a plausible suggestion. Towards the end of our second day Pieter Mostert and his contingent arrived and shared in our amazement and excitement. One of Pieter's assistants was crouching, gazing at the line of tracks through half closed eyes. Holding out his hands in front of him as though he was about to start walking on them, he said:
" Dis 'n ding wat hop – soos 'n kangaroo..." (It's a thing that hops – like a kangaroo...)

We took a unanimous decision to have this find protected in the best possible way. The

Eleven imprints could be identified in an ancient layer of silt

worst that could happen, we agreed, was a car driving across these tracks. So they were covered up with huge custom made metal boxes and the hope that nature would do its part by depositing a layer of wind blown sand on top of the site.

During the odd moment when I had looked up from brushing and sweeping the tracks I had noticed some things – probably stones – lying on the otherwise homogenous surface of sand a few hundred metres from our site. As a last concession before we were about to leave, I walked over to see what was actually lying on the ground over there. I picked up four isolated stones. To my utter amazement they could be fitted together to form an artefactual core! There were clean scars of flakes that had been removed before these last three flakes had been taken off, but there was no longer any sign of them on the surface. Even I did not have the gumption to suggest another excavation to find them below the surface…The technique according to which the flakes had been removed from this core implied a pre-Later Stone Age date at least. They might have been made as long as 150 000 years ago! Could they be related to the tracks?! It was impossible to say. Yet both discoveries represented two more tiny chips in the huge puzzle of our prehistory.

Further along and close to Tsondab Vlei and Sossus Vlei we picked up wonderful examples of hand axes, choppers and cleavers, stone flakes, chips and chunks, which were produced in the course of shaping the tools for hunting and gathering. These finds indicated that during Middle and Early Stone Age times the conditions in the Central Namib provided for those who were here before us.

I was absorbed and fascinated by the wealth of information I was discovering in connection with my assignment: reconstructing climatic conditions in the central Namib Desert.

Three stone flakes could be fitted onto an artefactual core, 12 cm in length (Photo Günther Komnik)

CHAPTER 9

MIRABIB HILL SHELTER IN THE CENTRAL NAMIB DESERT

On my first visit to the Mirabib Hill Shelter I spotted a clay pot cornered amongst the boulders just beyond the shelter's drip line. The moments of these rare and unexpected finds are unforgettable and stand out vividly against the background of all other happenings of the day, which fade away with time. The almost complete, bag shaped, black pot was lying on its side. There was nothing inside the pot. A thick layer of soot was adhering to the outside of the pot. Cradling this treasure in my lap on the drive back to the Research Station I remember day dreaming about the soot having been some kind of decoration since there was no trace of any kind of decoration on this vessel.

This was not unusual for pottery found in southwestern Africa, which was distinct from the earthenware found over the rest of the continent. Subconsciously I probably wanted to

Mirabib Hill Shelter

'upgrade' this pottery, which was technologically less sophisticated than the pottery associated with the Bantu-speaking societies in Africa. I – the equaliser, tending to side with the underdog hopelessly influenced by the western value system…

I spotted a clay pot hidden under a rock

Whatever my thoughts may have been the fact remained that "my" undecorated pot, with its pointed base, made of a coarse type of clay and with two lugs, was characteristic of this region and therefore a genuine product of the indigenous inhabitants of this area. Presently these were the !Naranin group of Nama (Khoekhoekowab) speaking people who are also referred to as the Topnaar. I was told that the Dutch syllables 'Top' and 'naar' implied being near (naar) the point/top of people on the move, coming from far away places. During the 19th century groups of Nama families were moving northwards from the cape with herds of small stock. But they were also hunting and gathering. From time to time, they may also have adopted the lifestyle of beachcombers or Strandlopers. Dotted along the banks of the Kuiseb River, place names and remnants of camps or settlements are testimony to a nomadic or semi-nomadic life style.

Gobabeb, one such place name, where the Namib Desert Research Station was established, was a case in point and the village of Sout Rivier or !u//aib a few kilometres further west, remains a good example of a village inhabited by Topnaar families. Johanna Fischer (born of a German father), a true matriarch, was an impressive personality as was Gerd Gariseb, the head of another household. They were a mine of information with regard to Topnaar traditions and the geography of the area. In becoming friendly with these neighbours of mine I was once again tempted to add the anthropology hat to my headgear of archaeologist, climatologist and palaeontologist.

The first records I made of the Mirbabib Hill shelter included photographs depicting the rock paintings. Monochrome figures of animals and people were fairly well preserved on a vertical slab of granite forming one of the walls of this large rock shelter.

Johanna Fischer cooking mieliepap   *Gerd Gariseb – a character*

The greater part of the shelter's surface was covered by a dung floor. Having grown up on a sheep farm no more than 200 kilometres north of Mirabib I was very familiar with the floor of sheep kraals. Although mildly surprised, I dismissed the observation with the mental note: "….. so people must have kept some sheep here at one point..." and then gradually I began to wonder: "Who?" I asked Johanna Fischer and Gerd Gariseb. They were vague about this. Well, who else if not the Topnaar or anyone whom they would have known? And then the question: "When?'

The most common and the most striking features recorded on the surface of the shelter consisted of microlithic artefacts – small stone tools – grinding stones, pestles and mortars – owl pellets, patches of ash and fire places.

The time had come to get down to some serious archaeological excavation. After surveying and mapping a trench was laid out at right angles to the back wall of the shelter beneath a rocky ledge where owls had been living for a long time. The 2x7 metre trench bisected the shelter into two almost equal portions.

My two assistants, Richard McWay-Wilson and his brother Michael were new to archaeology and amazed at my instructions of limiting the work of excavation to carefully and lightly brushing with paint brushes the fine, dry, dusty deposit before sifting it. Whatever stayed behind in the sieve had to be carefully scrutinised and then assigned to categories of material such as owl pellet remains, bone, plant remains, stone and stone artefacts.

Mirabib Hill Shelter before excavations started

Richard and Michael reacted to these tasks with an unending sense of humour and remarks like:

"You mean, we will be painting the desert with a narrow paint brush square millimeter by square millimeter?" Or:

"I thought my days in the sand pit were over..." or mixing incredulity with fun and peals of laughter.

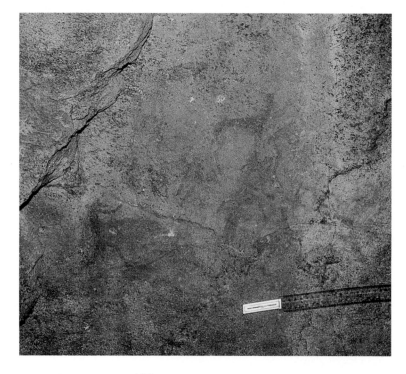

Rock paintings on a wall of Mirabib Hill Shelter

The loose deposit covering the dung floor could be swept away

"You want us to collect the turds?!"

"Every single one of them," was my reply with a straight face,
"theoretically the archaeologist should be able to reconstruct everything found in an excavation."

More seriously I added that the dung floor was really puzzling me.

"As though we don't have enough sh… around anyway," Richard commented dryly.

Michael had an endless string of jokes in store.

"What is red and sounds like a bell??"

"….D..u…u..ngggggg…" (tongue)

But the lightheartedness with which the days passed did not distract us from doing excellent work. The two young men fully understood what we were doing and we had ongoing, stimulating discussions about a vast range of topics. The experience with this twosome made me conclude that a good sense of humour was an essential ingredient of intelligence.

The first exciting result from specialists to whom I had submitted samples of the dung floor came from the Forensic Laboratory of the South African Police. The hair embedded in the dung floor was that of sheep. That took care of our speculations about stomach contents of oryx antelope having been used to create a living floor. It had been offered as one explanation for the dung floor and was based on the assumption that the stone implements indicated habitation of the shelter during a time before domesticated animals had arrived in the area.

Now our curiosity focussed on a date for this sheep dung floor. Since sheep herding was assumed to be a recent phenomenon one would have expected to find materials such as glass, porcelain or enamel ware, none of which had been found in direct association with the dung floor. What a surprise to receive a date of approximately 450 A.D. for sheep herding in the Namib Desert! At the time this was one of only three early dates for this important domesticate in southern Africa: Lynn Wadley had found the jaw bone of a sheep in the Erongo Mountains dated to approximately 200 A.D. and Frank Schweitzer at the Cape had found evidence of sheep even earlier than that, that is two thousand years ago.

The significance of the Mirabib date was enhanced by the evidence of herding versus the possible occasional 'catch' or theft of an individual animal. The dung floor implied rearing a number of sheep thus representing an important change in the people-animal relationship from hunting to stock-rearing.

Although we were a superb team of three our rate of progress was excruciatingly slow: one, or at most two layers 5 centimetres thick in a one metre square during a nine-hour day. Bearing in mind that we might be going for a depth of at least a metre in 14 squares this could mean a full year of uninterrupted digging! Aside from that, Michael was available only for the time of the University vacation and Richard could not devote himself to this project exclusively. Consequently I started looking for volunteers to assist me. With my princely salary of R175 per month there was no question of paying anyone for their services, which meant looking for true idealists.

The most appropriate assistants would have been the students I had been tutoring at the University of the Western Cape. We had talked about the work I was planning to do at Gobabeb and they had been fascinated. But the rules governing what 'white' (or blanke) people were allowed to do during the 1970's in Namibia, were very different from the rules pertaining to the so-called 'non-whites' (or nie-blankes). I suspected that my students would not be allowed to even enter a nature park. It was silly, but I tried to play a version of the game called "Try for White" on the pretext that I was unable to distinguish the hue of skin colour of the students.

So I submitted the names of four students to the authorities as I would submit the names of other (white) visitors. Their names were Afrikaans names and might just as well have belonged to 'whites'. But when the students arrived at the offices of the then Department of Nature Conservation in Windhoek to catch a ride with the next truck coming down to Gobabeb, I had an urgent radio call from an upset (white) official at the Windhoek office. This was long before the time of a telephone connection.
"Did you apply for a permit to have non-whites come and help you? Over."
"No, I did not, because these are university students and the best qualified helpers I can get to work free of charge. Over."
"But this is impossible. You know perfectly well that you do not even have separate toilets for them. Over."
"But we will not be at the station. We will be camping at Mirabib. Over."…..and OUT.
I was thus forced to look for other sources of help and activated my social network. My friend, Olga Levinson was hosting a radio programme 'Women's World' and launched an appeal for volunteers to get a taste of archaeological fieldwork in the Namib Desert. To my delight a steady stream of volunteers came to my rescue singly or in groups. This led to a series of intermittent spates of generally very pleasant fieldwork at the Mirabib Hill Shelter.

The interruptions in the process of excavation allowed me to review, sort and clearly label the finds and to start analysing and testing the observations made. There also was time to arrange for visits by experts in various fields who came to the Research Station from time to time. This led to several significant discoveries and provided invaluable lessons of all kinds. These stimulating personal contacts were extremely important in the otherwise isolated or even insulated daily life, which could be oppressive and debilitating at the Research Station in the middle of the Namib Desert. The quality of life there was determined by the synergy generated in the small population of Gobabeb.

Mary Seely, the boss-lady, as Michael and Richard called her rather affectionately, probably played the key role in this regard. Government Officials, representing the Department of Nature Conservation were transferred from time to time. Some of them were scientists in their own right. They would live at the station with their wives and children (note that a female official with husband and children had not yet been heard of...). They were the authoritative counterpart to Mary Seely, usually at odds with her about petty problems. Other residents or visiting scientists like myself rarely numbered more than three or four and Mary would have two or three assistants like Richard McWay-Wilson. The people who came to stay for various assignments would invariably be infatuated with the exotic surroundings of Gobabeb and with the research station. But apart from Mary Seely nobody managed to stay for an extended period of time.

AN ETHNO-ARCHAEOLOGICAL STUDY OF THE !NARANIN / TOPNAAR

The edible pips or seeds of the !Nara plant (*Acanthosicyos horridus*) were found throughout the Mirabib deposit down to a time-depth of over 8 000 years. They were aesthetically only slightly more pleasing than the turds making up the dung floor but at least as interesting in terms of providing information on the prehistoric economy of the inhabitants of the area.

Johanna Fischer collecting !nara on the creeper-like bushes growing on the dunes

For us as pupils at school in Walvis Bay or Swakopmund !naras were as popular as peanuts. But it took me half a lifetime to start realizing the peculiarities of this cucurbit, which is endemic to the Namib Desert. The creeper-like bushes covering the sand dunes have no leaves, only thorns.

After removing the skin from the melons the flesh was boiled and then Gerd Gariseb removed the seeds with a home-made sieve

The seeds were then dried on the roof of the house

The apparently endlessly long, adventitious roots looked more like stems of trees and stored a host of nutritious and medicinally significant substances. The flesh of the thorny fruit with a shape similar to the related 'tsamma' or honeydew melon, is extremely sweet. The seeds need only very little rain to germinate and will then thrive on the minimal humidity of the desert. The plants are salt tolerant and the young, soft shoots provide fodder for herbivores. In addition to this catalogue of features the !nara is prehistorically significant because we found evidence of it having been a staple food for no less than the past 8 000 years in the Namib Desert.

We tested this hypothesis by studying the breakage patterns of the pips. Although my recollection of the broken seed coats under the school desks was quite good I double-checked by studying a sample of seed coats collected from a Topnaar back yard and by comparing their appearance with the seed coats found in the excavation at the Mirabib Hill Shelter. In all these cases most of the seeds had been split along the seams of the oval flattish seed. Often there was a jagged rupture across one half of the seed coat. By contrast, seeds that we had put out for animals to feed on had either disappeared completely or tiny nibble marks were left on very small irregular fragments of seeds and seed coats.

The indication of a long tradition of people eating !nara seeds suggested that we study the living tradition. It would add to a better understanding of how people were relating to plants during Stone Age times before plants were domesticated. Apart from odd stories about the traditions of the !Naranin people no scientific reports were available. One of these tales related that the Topnaar were preparing the seeds for sale to whites by first eating and then excreting them.

On closer observation it turned out that when the sweet, yellow flesh adhering to the seeds dried, it turned black and made the seeds look dirty. Locals did not mind this because they liked the added, sweet flavour and they knew that it was not 'dirt' adhering to the seed coats. Whites, however requested the seeds to be "cleaned properly". This was done by boiling the fruit with the seeds for a long time until there was no flesh left on the seeds and thus they looked 'nice and clean'.

More information generated more work, in this case it was for my role of anthropologist and ethnologist. This task was made easier by teaming up with Ursula Dentlinger. She was one of the very few Namibian students taking Anthropology at the University of Cape Town. Ursula agreed to undertake an ethno-archaeological study of the Topnaar along the Kuiseb River. The idea was to compare her observations with findings from the excavation. It was a great pleasure working with Ursula who came to spend several months at Gobabeb. I had known her family and had heard about her long before I met her and discovered that she more than lived up to her wonderful reputation.

Together with Robbie Robinson who was working on his Master's degree in Botany and his friend, Alan Channing, yet another herpetologist also completing degree requirements, we were privileged to experience that exceptional rainy season of 1974 at Gobabeb when the Kuiseb River carried water for months on end. We would share tasks and help one another.

Unloading the !nara from the donkey cart

After a day of driving around the sand dunes on a Topnaar donkey cart, collecting ripe !nara we would spend the night along the banks of the Kuiseb River catching frogs. We were energised by continuous wit. The desert air would ring with peals of laughter. More often than not, one of us would land in the water while the frog leapt on to the river bank and went into hiding before one or other of his toenails had been clipped to mark that he was number x before he was let go again. Alan's study related the behaviour of frogs to time, temperature and humidity. This would explain how some reptiles could apparently anticipate rain. They were perceptive to changes in air pressure, temperature and humidity and thus the metereological conditions preceding rainfall. Tongue in cheek we related this esoteric information to rock paintings of snakes with ears. Such motifs were known in Namibia's rock art and we thus interpreted one of the many mysteries of the genre: snakes with ears meant that snakes could hear rain approaching.

Ursula Dentlinger's Honours thesis turned out to be an invaluable documentation on the role of the !nara in the traditional economy of the Topnaar. We wrote up a brilliant proposal on cultivating, utilizing and ultimately domesticating this fascinating plant. Every botanist and scientist who read our proposal, supported the project and we fantasised about eradicating poverty among the Topnaar. Sadly, however, we could not obtain the crucial logistic and financial support needed to implement our excellent plans. The Academy of Sciences in Washington only had funds for doing research on trees. However hard we tried to make the !nara look like a tree, the Academy turned down our proposal. When we submitted the proposal to the South African Government in the mid-seventies, they would only consider it on condition that we, as individuals, would resign from the project. Perhaps it related to my reputation of being a security risk. They were also not prepared to entertain any cooperation with 'outsiders' or persons who did not carry a South African passport.

So, in many ways, the political climate forced me to live life on a tight rope. Every step had to be carefully considered because it was so easy to be annihilated by either becoming destitute or socially unacceptable or both. The problem was compounded by having dreams about doing work that could lead to 'great things', be these discoveries about our history or prehistory, or by changing our social conditions from being oppressive and debilitating to becoming enlightened and enabling.

My relationship with Mary Seely had become strained and it was obvious that there was no future for me at the Namib Desert Research Station. I did not know where to go and what to do next. I was determined to carry on with the fieldwork programme I had designed but I needed a base from which to operate. Ursula's parents, Herman and Wilma, helped me out of this dilemma with the generous offer of a building on their farm Seeis, where I would be able to park equipment and material that I was working on. I would even be able to stay there if I wanted to, until my life became more stable. This immediate solution gave me a sense of security without which I might just have lost my mind. It enabled me to plan further field work and to proceed with the basic work of sorting and storing the finds that were accumulating in the course of the excavations.

GETTING TO KNOW PLANTS THROUGH THE MICROSCOPE

Apart from the interesting observations made in connection with the finds of the !nara kernels, I was struck by the excellent preservation of other plant material found in all the layers of the Mirabib deposit. This should be able to provide answers to questions about changes in the occurrence of plants near the shelter. Such changes might have been quantitative or qualitative. A greater abundance of one sort of wood in one layer than in another might reflect more trees of that sort having been around than at another time. Or it might be possible that some species had grown here a long time ago, which were no longer found in the area today. Both observations could reflect changes in climatic conditions.

The first step would have to be the identification of the plant remains found in the different layers. I approached one of the few qualified botanists working in the country at the time to ask whether it would be possible to identify plant species on the basis of the remains I was finding. The answer was yes, provided I could bring seeds or fruit, flowers and leaves of the plants I was finding! This was clearly utopia.

Doing archaeological work meant getting down on your hands and knees scraping, brushing, looking, checking, recognizing or guessing and deciding whether to pick up an object or not, whether to prepare it for a photograph by gentle sweeping or blowing or whether to chuck it into a bucket and then into the sieve. Fine loose material falls through the mesh and everything with dimensions exceeding the mesh size remains behind for once more being subjected to staring, comparing and attempting identification. It frequently happened that even the most basic kind of categorization – was it animal, vegetable or mineral - presented a problem. Where do you put a 'simple' turd? Assuming that it was produced by a herbivore it might make sense to put it together with faunal material. On the other hand the stomach content of ostriches has been analysed for the sake of identifying the plant species eaten by the animal. According to that point of view it might be put with plant material.

In any case the archaeologist has to concentrate up to the point of exhaustion when mind and/or eyes seize up and you realise that your brain has switched off! Then you stop, take a deep breath or some refreshment, relax – a good laugh does wonders – and recall that you are working with invaluable, uniquely precious material, which contains information that has not been recorded before. As scientific research is progressing, testing and analyzing all kinds of materials and discovering information from observations which had not been made previously, amazing insights are won. Before the wonders of radio carbon dating were discovered archaeologists would hardly have considered collecting charcoal. I once imagined a machine being invented, which would x-ray an archaeological deposit and be able to observe all sorts of fascinating details which cannot be preserved by our rather crude methods of excavation. That was one good reason for disturbing only as small a section as possible of any archaeological deposit and for ensuring that the remaining portion be preserved as completely as possible for future, more sophisticated investigation.

Such thoughts would end a short break and get me back to studying the residue in the sieve. The bulk of what was left behind in the sieve generally consisted of plant matter. I started dealing with it by designing categories which I thought made sense. Seeds, in particular !nara seeds, were easy to pick out. Then there were other seeds, pieces of tree bark, leaves, fragments of stems, twigs or branches, charcoal and pieces of wood, which could be distinguished from one another with the naked eye.

When we had sorted a sample of plant material from every main layer in the excavation I went to the herbarium in Pretoria and asked for advice. They showed me techni-colored microscope slides of sections of plant tissue, which struck me as beautiful!

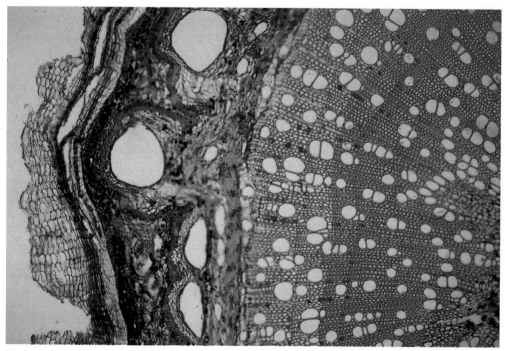

Thin section of stem of Commiphera saxicola seen through the microscope (greatly enlarged) (National Botanical Institute Pta)

Then I learned that each colour represented a different kind of cell and that every species of plant had its very own fingerprint or pattern in which its cells were arranged. In other words a small piece of wood – charcoal would even be better – could tell me that it came, for example from an *Acacia erioloba*, that is the camel-thorn tree! I was thrilled. Even a small plastic bag of plant material from a single layer in the excavation contained enough information to say which plants had accumulated there during a certain period of time. That would give an idea about what was growing in the area.

In theory I soon grasped what needed to be done for me to obtain this information. In practice it meant a great deal of hard work and acquiring skills I certainly did not have. Once again a good friend of mine came to my rescue. Gerhild Gmeiner was a medical technologist with a spirit of adventure and a good sense of humour. When I told her how small bits of plant would have to be embedded in wax and then cut into slices thin enough to be transparent under the microscope, she exclaimed:
"I can do that. That is precisely what we do in histology. I have embedded human tissue in wax and I can work with a micrometer. And you know that I would love to spend time with you in the field."
Her enthusiasm was contagious and we swiftly arranged for her to spend some time with me at Gobabeb selecting the material, which we would then prepare for the microscopic work in the laboratory of the Windhoek hospital. The production of the first successful slide of a piece of stem that had been hardened in a tiny block of wax, cut and stained in different colours before being fixed in between the two glass covers of the microscope slide called for celebration. It was so pretty.

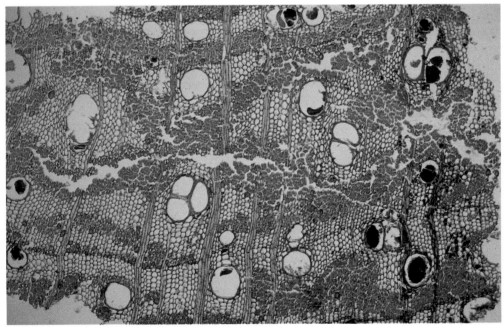

Thin section of a bit of plant material found at Mirabib (greatly enlarged) identified as Acacia erioloba

But what was it? The Pretoria Herbarium had given me a number of microscope slides with sections of reliably identified plant species. Now we would have to find a match for our archaeological material with a slide of the identified specimens. In this way we became familiar with plant species which I had not yet met personally out in the wilderness.

It was also becoming clear that we would have to produce our own key of microscope slides for the plants growing in the vicinity of the Mirabib Hill Shelter at present. Ernest (Robbie) Robinson had been working on an inventory of plants in the central Namib Desert and this was the invaluable basis and start of our work. But it did not consist of microscope slides. It consisted of a list of approximately 120 names and of herbarium sheets with samples of dried plants, which we were not allowed to tamper with. Therefore we had to go out and collect samples of plants, ideally seeds, fruit, leaves, flowers and wood, stick them onto our own herbarium sheets, compare them with the identified specimens to verify our correct identification and then snip off the bits we wanted to dissect and preserve as microscope slides.

One day while we were sitting in the laboratory at Gobabeb we had a visit of Professors Walter and his wife Erna Walter. Both of them were botanists of international fame who had contributed substantially to the knowledge of Namibian flora. They were very interested in what we were doing and invited me to visit the ethno-botanical research unit at Stuttgart's Hohenheim University. I was particularly impressed by one of their comments: "What you have started here is work for a life time – see that it does not get lost."

I did not have a life time to spend on the plant remains of Mirabib. So I decided to limit my report on this work by describing the techniques we were using. Samples of our work would serve to illustrate the potential of applying these techniques more elaborately. For the time being our work supported and reflected the general conclusions about cycles of climatic change in the central Namib Desert.

OWL PELLETS AS INDICATORS OF CLIMATIC CHANGE

A young barn owl living at the Makapan Limeworks in South Africa (Photo: C.K. Brain)

The indigestible parts of owls' food were found in every layer of the excavation. The nest of a barn owl was situated in a crevice of the shelter's wall right above the trench we were excavating. Barn owls feed during the night in an area with a radius of about 12 kilometres from their roost. Once back home they regurgitate their prey and produce these veritable nuggets containing insect remains, skeletal parts of small rodents, birds and reptiles all stuck together in oblong pellets two to three centimetres long. As the binding saliva dries up, the pellets disintegrate, but the diagnostic little bones and insect fragments are preserved in the deposit and contain information on the changing environment over millennia. We carefully collected and labelled the remnants of what owls had eaten according to the layers in which they were found.

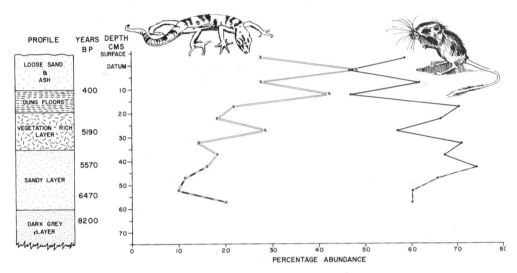

Graph representing the results of the owl pellet analysis

The palaeontologist takes over from there and identifies the species of animals on which the owls fed. When Dr Brain, well-known South African palaeontologist and the Director of the Transvaal Museum in Pretoria, explained the process of identifying the teeth of rodents to me I was incredulous. It involved studying the pattern of cusps on the molars of mice teeth! This highly specialised study made it possible to say that a certain kind of animal was living in the vicinity of Mirabib during the time when a particular layer of material had accumulated in the shelter. With carbon 14 dating of organic material the age of the layer could be determined. Since the layers proved to be thousands of years old a margin of error even of decades was negligible.

Dr Bob Brain had started collecting owl pellets that were currently accumulating in a narrow rock gorge on the Mirabib Mountain a few kilometres west of the Mirabib Hills shelter. Together with his daughter Virginia he observed that the pellets collected during droughts reflected a different owl menu from those, which were collected during periods with good rainfall. The drought menu consisted exclusively of insects and small reptiles like geckos and lizards. During good rain years the pellets would contain the bones of small mammals such as ground squirrels, mice and rats.

These creatures withdrew from the gravel plains of the Namib during dry periods to live in the riverine forests along the Kuiseb River. In other words, layers, which contained owl pellets without the remains of small mammals, represented dry periods and vice versa. The layers in which the owl pellets contained skeletal remains of rats and mice indicated moister conditions.

In the course of studying the owl pellet remains collected at Mirabib, Bob and his daughter, Virginia Brain also were on the lookout for teeth belonging to that recently re-discovered insectivore, the Golden Mole (*Eremitalpa granti namibensis*), which is endemic to the sand dunes. This species was conspicuously absent from the pellets accumulating at Mirabib Mountain, indicating that the owls nowadays did not reach the dune area. Should the archaeological deposit at Mirabib contain teeth of the Golden Mole this might mean that the dunes had been closer to the shelter than they are today. This was therefore another question put the analysis of the owl pellets: did the dunes cross the bed of the Kuiseb River during some time in the past while people were occupying the Mirabib Hill Shelter? The absence of Golden Mole bones or teeth in the owl pellets found at the Mirabib Hill Shelter therefore indicated that the sand dunes had not crossed the riverbed during the past eight thousand years.

" It would really be nice to find a site with owl pellet remains in another deposit here in the Namib. Then we could compare the findings," Bob said to me on one of his visits to the Research Station. This remark led to excavations at Hennops Cave and Charè, two sites approximately equidistant from Mirabib. Hennops Cave was part of a large underground lime-stone formation north-east of Mirabib and on the farm Charè there was another rock shelter south-east of Mirabib.

Accounts of archaeological work are invariably highlighted by the carbon 14 dates obtained from samples of charcoal or other organic material submitted for dating to specialised laboratories. This process may take months and anxiety has a good chance of building up during this time. The dates received for the excavation at Mirabib caused due excitement because they pinpointed an unprecedented time sequence for climatic changes in the central Namib Desert during the Holocene, the most recent epoch in earth history covering 10 000 years. I was particularly pleased about this because the Mirabib data fitted into that void of time following on after the finds of Early Stone Age tools in the dune Namib.

I had started off with the fundamental question: Has the Namib environment *always* been as it is today? A clear *no* to this question had already been provided by the fossils, which Gudrun Corvinus had found at Arrisdrift, an ancient site on the Orange River. Animals requiring humid conditions had lived there some 30 million years ago. They were extinct by now but the fossil remains of *Elephas reckii* in the dunes south of the Kuiseb did not indicate desert conditions either during the late Pleistocene. During these times early *Homo* was starting to shape the first stone tools. Perhaps the Swakop River entered the Atlantic Ocean via an estuary at that time. The fossilised oyster shells we had found between Walvis Bay and Swakopmund would fit into that picture as well.

The next point in the calendar would be indicated by the 23 000 year old snail shells found in the mud layers of Homeb. By then *Elephas reckii* and likely ancestors of our race namely *Homo erectus* and early *Homo sapiens* would have withdrawn from the ever drier central Namib. The Kuiseb River would have ended in a vlei or pond similar to present day Sossus or Tsondab Vlei. Mirabib Hill Shelter might have attracted only occasional hunting expeditions. The hunters left behind no more than a few quartz flakes in the soft, red sand covering the shelter floor.

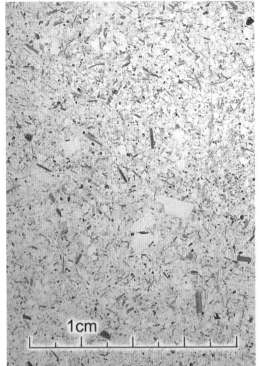 

A thin section of the basal red sand found at Mirabib looked at under the microscope shows hardly any organic material contained in the deposit (Photo: H. Scholz)

A thin section of the dark grey layer shows bone (top left) and charcoal implying a high content of organic material by comparison with the red sandy layer below it (Photo: H. Scholz)

Then conditions changed once more and the dark-grey layer, which produced a radio carbon date of 6200 B.C. accumulated. It obtained its colour from an abundance of ash and charcoal, which implies intensive habitation with enough wood available for making many fires. Microscopic slides of pieces of charcoal were identified as *Acacia erioloba* wood.

A small granite grinding stone with a film of red colour covering its smooth hollow surface was one of the most exciting finds from this layer and might be connected to the red paintings on the wall of the shelter. A picture of fat years in the central Namib Desert emerged: regular rain – not necessarily in vast quantities – herds of game – a good supply of food from the veld – sufficient fresh water stored in the beautiful granite basins of Mirabib Hill and springs a little further off in the Gorob canyon or even the Kuiseb River – pleasant climate and leisure time for socializing and creative expression...

Two thousand years later, however, conditions had once more deteriorated and prevented permanent habitation of the shelter. A date of roughly 4500 B.C. was obtained from a fireplace in Mirabib's thick sandy layer and indicated occasional visits to the shelter, probably during good rainy seasons. The owl pellet remains indicate conditions conducive to such seasonality. Although the plant remains in this layer showed a remarkable decrease in quantity compared to those found in the dark-grey layer they nevertheless represented less arid conditions than those reflected in the sterile red sand covering the bedrock.

The layer on top of this central sandy layer was once more characterised by much more plant material and a sample of charcoal was dated to approximately 3000 B.C. It was awesome to consider these dates in perspective with the concepts of old and ancient as generally applied. In school the birth of Jesus Christ was almost identified with the beginning of time. Anything that had happened Before Christ was definitely very old or ancient. Trying to imagine people living in the Mirabib Hill Shelter eight thousand years ago – and anywhere else in Namibia for that matter – demanded mental leaps.

When did the first sheep appear in Namibia? Or in southern Africa? Domestication of wild species was said to have started in Asia Minor and Egypt approximately ten thousand years ago. Archaeologists working in those areas were talking about the Neolithic period. How did communities start to become sedentary and to live together in greater numbers leading to the development of complex social structures and social stratification? With regard to Africa these phenomena were relegated to the Iron Age and it was assumed that Iron Age features spread into sub-Saharan Africa with the migration of Bantu-speaking peoples from north, west or central Africa. With regard to south-western Africa – let alone South West Africa alias Namibia we were only starting to formulate relevant questions. The dung floor presented utterly exciting evidence. The C 14 date of approximately 450 A.D. was matched with finds of sheep hair embedded in this layer. These fascinating results drew the attention of the entire, tiny world of archaeologists in southern Africa.

Unfortunately the atmosphere in that tiny world was not always inspiring. The exciting time at Gobabeb ended on a bitter note. Luckily I had been offered a temporary one year position as lecturer at the University of Cape Town, which I could take up because of the Dentlingers who had offered me the base at Seeis. In Cape Town, while teaching, I could write up the monograph entitled 'Mirabib - an archaeological study in the Namib Desert'. Colleagues studied the manuscript and I conscientiously weighed up every comment they had made. My sincere appreciation for the time and trouble they had taken was expressed in a page of acknowledgements. It therefore came as a shock to be viciously attacked, after the report had been published, by a small group of individuals working in Namibia. They criticised sampling methods of plant material, stylistic elements and aspects of my personality. When one of them walked past me in the street without greeting I stopped in my tracks and called out to him:
"Hey, did you not see me?!"
He turned around and said that he could no longer associate with someone whose work was of such a low standard as mine. Another one dropped to the level of writing nasty anonymous letters to the editor of a Windhoek newspaper. This was a bitter lesson in realizing that good science is not without unscientific rubbish. A precious circle of truly wonderful friends helped me in dealing with these unexpected expressions of antagonism. One of the most delightfully liberating insights came from my cherished colleague, Dr Brain:
"It is not only about the pure pursuit of truth, " he said and then added,
"It could be, if human primates were not involved."
"What then would be preferable?" I asked.
"If we, as animals with mental insights into so many things, could have come from good carnivore stock, instead of from the devious primates," he went on.
Perhaps that is why they became so dominant?

The next few years were spent on determined efforts to continue with my research on climatic change - and on making a living. A manuscript, with results of field work following up on what had been done at Mirabib, was not accepted for publication in the government funded MADOQUA where 'Mirabib' had been published. In the prevailing political climate I suspected that this was due to the reputation of me being a spy, activist and clandestine member of SWAPO the South West Africa People's Organisation instrumental in bringing about Namibian Independence in 1990.

While I was teaching at the University of Cape Town I had another offer to work at the University of the Western Cape. It came to naught when I was accused of being a Russian spy. In the paranoid South Africa of that time this suspicion may have been due to the fact that I had changed from my married name 'Pendleton' back to my maiden name 'Sandelowsky'.

I kept trying to convince influential people of the importance of doing research on past climates on the preservation of our fragile environment on discovering the limitations of our underground water reserves and on coming to terms with the carrying capacity of a desert country. Apart from sincerely believing in this mission I thought that these were 'politically safe' topics. But I was wrong. I did manage to inspire some people. One of them belonged to the far right wing of the ruling party of the time. He admitted that if his colleagues were to overhear our conversations he would loose his job. In spite of that he was brave enough to secure another year's grant for me to continue with the work I had started at Gobabeb. There were no strings attached and I was not tied down in time or space. Retrospectively it was amazing what a grant of R7,500 allowed me to do in the course of a little more than a year - with the support of a wonderful group of friends. They made their 4x4 cars available to me for fieldwork, they worked like galley slaves in the field they bought food when I ran out and most importantly, cheered me up when I was about to despair.

One of my survival tactics consisted of offering informal tuition in just about every skill I had acquired during my long years of study. Tiny adverts in a local daily were free of charge and I managed to set up evening classes in my two room flat for three to five individuals each in spoken English and German; in anthropology and archaeology. The cash income paid for food and rent. More importantly, friendships developed with many of my 'students'. Some of them inadvertently graduated to field assistants in due course.

From left to right: Alan Channing, Beatrice Sandelowsky, Ursula Dentlinger on the bank of the Kuiseb River in 1974

CHAPTER 10

MANAGING WITH THE HELP OF MY FRIENDS

I was firmly committed to continuing with archaeological research in Namibia. I wanted to find evidence relating, reflecting or in some way confirming the findings which had been published in the Mirabib report. I would have liked some more information on the prehistoric inhabitants themselves. Excavations at the Charè rock shelter and in the deep, underground Hennops cave seemed to offer the most promising results in connection with finding similar strata containing faunal, floral and anthropomorphic material. I was once more looking for voluntary help. Two of the students taking evening classes offered not only their free time, but also their 4x4 vehicles.

Charè Shelter

The Kuiseb River terrace with the red sand dunes spilling onto the river bed from the south and the walls of the canyon rising above the northern bank

have been a settlement with hut structures and stock enclosures. Brushing away loose sand on a darker patch of ground I found some charcoal. This could have been a fireplace. Probably not very old, I thought. But you never know. So I took a sample for carbon 14 dating.

Penny Borroughs records that the base of cairn A measured 5 metres across

Then I decided to excavate the largest cairn in the row of eight conical stone arrangements located along the edge of the canyon wall on the terrace east of the Gorob river. At its base this stone arrangement measured five meters in diameter.

We photographed and carefully plotted on graph paper every rock that could be seen on the surface before gradually dismantling precisely one half of this pile of stones. These were mostly slabs of mica-schist and quartzite, some of them too large to be lifted by any one of us alone. All along I cautioned that there might be finds as small as ostrich eggshell beads which would have to be recorded according to their precise location, preferably before touching them; or bits of fragile bone or something we could not even imagine. Speculations ran wild and kept us going in spite of several very hot hours in the middle of the day although we had picked the coldest season of the year for working there. On a few mornings we found that the nightly fog on our sleeping bags had turned to ice.

After no significant finds had been made in the course of lifting one half of the dissected cairn, the other half was also removed. The natural surface on which these stones had been lying consisted of fine sand, which formed the river terrace. A square one metre by one metre was marked out over the central part or core of the cairn and was carefully brushed (or painted) down in horizontal layers. Special care was taken to keep the four walls vertical and to avoid stepping too close to the edge. At a depth of approximately 80 centimetres it became very awkward to get in and out of the pit for all except Jens and Rudolf with their long legs.

I was getting a bit tense about the prospect of having hit upon a stone cairn that was not covering anything of interest, but may have been symbolizing or signifying something which no amount of digging would be able to identify. The conversation among my team members turned to fantastic stories about hidden treasures and wild mysteries. I expected to be told that the hole now was too deep to be continuing with the work. Instead, I was asked on which side of the test square we should extend the excavation so that a step could be formed to facilitate getting in and out.

I was very pleasantly surprised because I had feared a dampening of spirits. This might have led to a depressed atmosphere that would cause irritability. It would have been hard to insist on anything being done, let alone being done properly, like for instance, backfilling the pit and replacing the stones. I abandoned the time-consuming task of sifting the sterile sand and concentrated on paying careful attention to any change that might be occurring in the texture or colour of the deposit.

Within the next two days the method of extending the original one metre square had led to an excavation of 3 metres x 4 metres with a depth of 1.75 metre. We got in and out by stepladder (see book cover). With more than two persons in the pit every movement had to be carefully controlled because the collapse of one of the walls would have been a disaster.

On one cold, early morning three of us had stepped down to continue with the laborious task of scraping together neat little piles of sand into buckets which would be lifted up onto the step ladder to be emptied 'outside' or 'on top'. Suddenly there was a commotion 'outside'. All I remember seeing was a snake slithering towards the excavation, over the edge and into the pit! We have never been able to reconstruct how three adults got out of

147

a deep hole like that with only one step ladder in what seemed like a split second without destroying the neat vertical walls of the excavation - but they did!

Amongst shouting and laughing and throwing stones at the snake, I thought this might be the right time to admit defeat and to gracefully call it a day and close my report with some comment on sterile sand. I went to fetch the mid-morning snack from the car and started to pour tea from the thermos flasks. Then I presented my little closing down speech. It was met with silence.

Then Jens Schneider piped up and announced that he had a dream according to which we would be finding a skeleton. I was silent. The dream was discussed. Jens and Rudolf moved away from the group and talked very seriously. The rest of us sipped our tea with mixed feelings. Then the two young men came back with the following proposition: "Beatrice, please let the two of us dig any way we want for a while. If nothing has happened by sunset, we promise to refill the hole and to start packing so that we can leave in the morning."

What could I say? Why not? I fetched my camera and took a few shots of the neat piece of very level, sterile sand almost two metres below the natural surface. Then I withdrew into the meagre shade of a salvadore bush and started cleaning up my notes. Oliver had finally managed to take his mother to look at the home of some mice he had discovered in the riverbed. Penny and Cathy had gone back to camp to prepare lunch.

I cannot remember how much time had passed before I looked up in the direction of the excavation and saw Rudolf's head appearing over the edge. He motioned to me with his finger to come over. I was not in the mood for some prank, but I did also not want to be a spoilsport. Karin was sitting inside the pit smiling from ear to ear. Jens was lying flat on his stomach and it looked as though he had lost his right arm. To say I was puzzled would have been an understatement.
"They have actually found something," Karin said.
I climbed down the ladder. Jens pulled his arm out of a hole the opening of which was not much bigger than that of a shirt sleeve.
"You must lie down flat like I did and then just put your arm down the hole and feel," he said with a grin and a mischievous twinkle in his eyes.
I looked around for any disturbance and then did as I was told. And I had serious trouble believing what I felt.
" A..? Two...?! What?"
"Two bones!" the three of them echoed.
"Leg bones?"
"Arm bones?!"
"Definitely long bones....!"
Penny and Cathy must have been attracted by the mounting tension. Suddenly they were there.

Work continued until darkness fell. Without any effort I slipped back into my role of disciplinarian and insisted on gradually lowering the surface by moving from the corners of the pit towards the 'arm hole', which was about dead centre. By midmorning the next day we could detect a difference in the texture of the soil where the grave shaft had been dug. Very carefully we removed the less compacted deposit from the inside of an oval area

Karin Lubisch and Jens Schneider carefully removing the loose sand from inside the grave shaft

measuring 95 centimetres by 50 centimetres across. Before long the paint brushes swept open some bone. Now we took turns scooping out the sand (with spoons) from amongst the bones without moving them. At one point the driver of the truck came over and exclaimed:

" ...but this looks so professional..."

"...it looks so professional...."

Indeed it did. A skeleton was lying on its side in foetal position with the head resting on four large, white quartz stones. The only grave goods consisted of ostrich egg shell beads found amongst the ribs. The bones were in excellent condition and would thus be a joy for the physical anthropologist to analyse.

!Narob is situated downstream from the Kuiseb River canyon on the rocky plains north of the Kuiseb River

It did take another day before we were ready to move on to the last site of this trip further down stream and beyond the canyon of the Kuiseb River to a place called !Narob. A smaller stone cairn was identified and turned out to cover a crevice in the rocks, which almost looked like a stone sarcophagus - or part of one. Here we found another flexed skeleton. A piece of fibrous plant matter was lying next to the body, curved around the feet of the skeleton.

What looked like a !Nara root curved around the feet of the skeleton

Could this be a part of !nara plant root?! Ursula and I had once excavated a !nara plant growing amongst the granite rocks close to the riverbed. Its roots were miserable specimens compared to the trunk-like roots of the plants growing in the dunes. A large !nara root like the one found next to the skeleton would not have grown naturally on such a rocky surface as presented in this grave. It is suggested that this !nara root was placed next to the skeleton as an indication of the importance of this staple to the inhabitants of the area – the !Naranin – the people of the !nara. It would qualify as grave goods.

!Nara root growing on rocky surface

!Nara root growing in the sand

151

The work we did during the 1977 field season was rewarded with significant results. The skeleton of the Gorob Mouth cairn was that of a healthy, young man while the !Narob skeleton had belonged to an older man. The !nara (*Acanthosicyos horridus)* root with a C 14 date of approximately 300 A.D. buried with him might have been a tribute to a super !nara collector or cook almost two thousand years ago!

The sample of charcoal taken from what had looked like an old fire place at the Gorob River mouth site had a date of approximately 800 A.D. A third date of about 1 300 A.D. for a skeleton found beneath another stone cairn on the gravel plains just north of Gorob River mouth fitted in with these two dates. I related these finds to the date of ± 450 A.D. for the sheep dung floor at Mirabib. The acquisition of domesticated animals could imply greater material wealth promoting concepts of power and status in the society. Although there were quite a number of stone cairns along the edge of the Kuiseb river it could be assumed that not every individual would have been buried in such an elaborate fashion. Possibly these stone cairns marked the graves of persons with special status.

The three years at Gobabeb had been the longest period I had stayed in one place since my High School days and yet they had passed too swiftly to have served as a time for consolidation or stabilization. At least I had stayed on the same continent and most of the time in the same country. It now started to look as though the career options in this country and on this continent were too limited for an archaeologist specializing in the palaeo-ecology of the central Namib Desert. I warned myself against becoming a victim of my own specialization. Being an anthropologist belonging to the species praised for versatility and the ability to adapt to rapidly changing conditions, it would be a shame if I could not survive, I told myself.

My priorities were determined by my love of freedom, my desire to live and work in Namibia and the ambition of applying the skills and knowledge I had managed to acquire. I was aware of so many possibilities and needs that existed here, but was frustrated because I lacked the basic means of applying myself. Perhaps I should look for a job at a foreign institution and try to work from there. With that motive in mind I accepted an invitation to a conference of the L.S.B. Leakey Foundation in London in 1977. Contacts with colleagues working on bio-archaeology at the University of Groningen in Holland and at the Ethno-botanical Research Unit of the University of Hohenheim in Stuttgart led to an extended trip to London and the Continent. In retrospect this trip was the best way of spending the last cent of the grant facilitated by my friend in the Administration of S.W.A.

I was warmly welcomed at the Institute of Bio-archaeology in Groningen and saw how a great deal of ground breaking research could be done by a few qualified hard working people with limited space at their disposal. Under the microscope they were sorting and comparing seeds and other plant remains from archaeological excavations in Europe and Asia. There was a bone library consisting of the identified skeletal parts of a wide range of animals. Here an unidentified piece of bone could be compared with the most likely key specimen. Professor van Zeist also reassured me about visiting Dr Udelgard Körber-Grohne, ethno-botanist at the University of Hohenheim and I learned a great deal there as well. It became absolutely clear to me that the next important step in my archaeo-botanical work would consist of compiling a key to the flora of the central Namib. In my discussions with these experts I also realised how lucky I was to be working in the Namib Desert where plant life was limited to only one to two hundred species. Anywhere else the task facing me would have been hopelessly too big for an individual to take on.

At the beautifully organised Leakey Conference in London I met my Professors Desmond Clark, Glynn Isaac and Brian Fagan as well as other famous palaeontologists and archaeologists. They dissuaded me from leaving Namibia. I was just about the only person left in SWA/Namibia through whom anyone from outside could or might try to do some research or get some information about conditions in the country. United Nations Resolution 435 had just been passed and my mentors encouraged me to return to Namibia and to prepare for Independence! As a token for support I was awarded a grant of US$175 per annum by Professor Ned Munger of the L.S.B. Leakey Foundation.

On my return to Namibia I was pleasantly surprised to find that U.N. Resolution 435 was already being implemented. South Africa had appointed Judge M. T. Steyn as Administrator-General (A.G.) to prepare SWA/Namibia for Independence in the space of one calendar year. Contrary to my expectations Theunie Steyn was an enlightened and charming man who not only condoned new ideas but enthusiastically supported the ones he liked as best as he could. He introduced me to the management of the Rössing Uranium Ltd., the largest Uranium Mine in the world. I believe that he recommended me as an anthropological consultant and they appointed me. Although my advice was not always taken seriously, it was a nice change to be treated with respect and to have an income. The other great advantage was, that I had the freedom to organise my time, although a good part of it was now taken up with duties, which were removed from my archaeological work.

I managed to continue with the quest for data with which to compare the findings at Mirabib. While the stratification at Charè nicely corroborated the work at Mirabib, we had not found owl pellet remains in similar quantities. Bob Brain's words kept ringing in my ears "...It would really be nice to find another stratified site with owl pellet remains here in the Namib...."

HENNOPS CAVE

Justin Wilkinson, a student of geology, was doing prospecting work in the Namib Desert for a mining company. On a visit to Gobabeb he had told us about a deep underground limestone cave south of the Swakop River north east of Mirabib.
"I could not detect any obvious signs of human occupation," he told me,
"but there was an owl living in there which gave me quite a fright as it flew towards me out of the dark," he added with a laugh. I took that comment to indicate owl pellets in the cave. When Bob Brain was back at Gobabeb shortly thereafter we went to look at the site. It was agreed that it would be worthwhile to test the deposit.

We discussed the infra-structure that would be needed if I was going to do an excavation there. Justin thought that his Company would be supportive of such work and that we would be able to stay at the miners' camp. In addition the mine provided the equipment needed to light up the cave as well as the pulley to move buckets of excavated material from down below to the surface up above.

Only three years had passed since I had failed to get students from the University of the Western Cape to help me excavate at Mirabib on account of their racial identity as assigned according to Apartheid philosophy. In the meantime people in Namibia had come to accept political developments in the international arena and United Nations Resolution 435 was on everybody's lips. Leslie Maasdorp and his fellow students had graduated and

Dr Brain (right) at the entrance of Hennops Cave

were teaching in Rehoboth. Yes, four of them still were keen to come and work with me during the Easter vacation of 1978. I did not even have to apply for a special permit for them to enter the Namib Naukluft Park!

Author Beatrice Sandelowsky, Leslie Maasdorp and Hans-Karl Rügheimer inside Hennops Cave

Three more students from the evening classes joined the four students from Rehoboth. One of them, Karin Weber, belonged to that small group of women in Namibia who seemed to be suspect on account of their intelligence and their readiness to bridge the racial divides. Similarly Hans-Karl Rügheimer and Kuno Baedecker as males represented the exception rather than the rule of enlightened whites in the society.

In terms of artefactual finds there was not much to write home about at Hennops. A few bits of broken beer bottle and remnants of a small fire implied some very recent human activity. Nothing more of the kind was found below the surface of the soft deposit into which we were digging. Here we found thin slices of alternating coarse and fine sand containing rich quantities of owl pellet remains. We collected them according to the depth at which they were found. Again Dr Brain identified the tiny skeletal fragments and found that they reflected a similar pattern of occurrence as was found at Mirabib. The preservation of the material was good and this indicated that it would be worth time and effort to continue with work at this site.

The team spirit was terrific and all practical problems were solved amid jokes and laughter. One such problem concerned the creation of a patch of shade during the hottest part of the day when the sun was almost directly overhead. The suggestion of having lunch while lying down flat underneath the vehicles was not accepted. Instead we fastened some netting, an umbrella and a piece of canvas to the roofs of the cars standing next to one another. This gave us a sort of passage with just enough room for a small table and chairs.

Conversations revolved around the burning issues of the times: imminent Independence - Apartheid - education - how to best apply the resources that were available. I reported on my trip to Europe and Great Britain and the suggestion by my mentors to set up an organisation that would facilitate research in the country. Under the South African regime it had been all but impossible to obtain permission to do independent scientific work in SWA. Invariably we ended up talking about the problems we were most familiar with: the education system and discrimination. Rehoboth at that time was the second largest urban settlement in the country. There were ten schools in the town and about twice as many farm and village schools in the surroundings. There were at least 200 teachers in the area. Yet the only 'library' consisted of a few shelves of books at the Roman Catholic Mission Station. Other educational or even recreational facilities like museums, shows or parks were unheard of.

By the end of the two weeks at Hennops we had resolved to establish an educational organisation, to produce a feasibility study for setting up a library in Rehoboth and for designing an administrative structure to promote our plans.

Karin Weber

Creating shade where there is none

CHAPTER 11

THE UNIVERSITY CENTRE FOR STUDIES IN NAMIBIA (TUCSIN)

On 15 June 1978 the launch of THE UNIVERSITY CENTRE FOR STUDIES IN NAMIBIA (TUCSIN) was hosted in a rented colonial style building known as the REMMER CLINIC in the centre of Windhoek. Dr Ernst Scherz and his wife, Anneliese, who had just published the first ever comprehensive survey of PREHISTORIC ROCK ART IN NAMIBIA were among the guests at this historic occasion.

Dr Scherz wrote up the following report: (translated from German by the author)

GET-TOGETHER ON THE EVENING OF 15 JUNE 1978

occasioned by the move of Dr Sandelowsky's organisation into the upper storey of the Remmer Clinic.

"When my wife and I appeared in the rooms of the new institute shortly after 18h30 a number of prominent and intellectually oriented persons were already present. In the course of the evening the space would fill up considerably. I saw many old friends and many new faces whose acquaintance I was very pleased to make.

The fact that there were sufficient numbers of chairs to sit on marked a significant and welcome difference to otherwise similar launches hosted by the Arts Association. This facilitated the formation of continually changing groups in serious conversation. Thus it was easy for me to make meaningful contacts with numerous people.

This very interesting event focused on two speeches. Ms Rockstroh spoke about the history of the Remmer Clinic and Dr Sandelowsky talked about the aims and objectives of TUCSIN. Her presentation was received most sympathetically and it seemed that everyone was convinced of the urgent need for her work. A number of responses indicated this and expressed the sincere wish that the public as well as the authorities in power would support this initiative.

The fact that this day coincided with the birthday of Dr Sandelowsky gave the event a festive nature. Flowers and little gifts gave the otherwise plain room a merry look. Biscuits, cheese and wine were partaken of sparingly. In spite of the birthday the atmosphere remained austere and serious. In accordance with the intellectual calibre of those present the evening was of a high standard.

It can only be wished that beautiful development will follow up on this beautiful beginning."

The move mentioned by Dr Scherz referred to the movement of my material from the Farm Seeis to the Remmer Clinic.

I had hoped to persuade the managers of Rössing Uranium Ltd to support the ideas that were developing for TUCSIN but they rejected the prospect of promoting higher academic education, let alone archaeological research. But the idea of providing a facility for promoting basic education for underprivileged Namibians did take. Under the auspices of TUCSIN we drew up a proposal outlining an informal education programme for the Rössing Foundation. Literacy training and Basic English were offered as a start. This was accepted by the Board of the newly established Rössing Foundation. They agreed to rent an outbuilding of the Remmer Clinic as an office to start recruiting students for the courses we were going to offer.

Jerry Tobias was one of the students who had heard about TUCSIN and was looking for a scholarship. He had also applied for a job at Rössing and I was delighted when Rössing appointed him to assist me in setting up an Education Centre. On our first morning at the 'new' office in the outbuilding of the Remmer Clinic we found two desks and two chairs with a telephone that was not yet connected. For the sake of deciding on our priorities we went out and bought a kettle and two cups to make tea. While we were having our first tea break an ice cream seller (on a bicycle) approached our office. He had heard that lessons were going to be offered at this place. For what could he sign up? Literacy and English. Free of charge. He signed up. We were thrilled and reassured ourselves that this was going to be a great success. Within a few weeks we had registered enough students to start up classes in Literacy and English.

Efforts to find funds for TUCSIN to pay the rent for the main building of the Remmer Clinic on the other hand, had failed dismally. Not everyone in the group, which had attended our pretty little inauguration, felt strongly enough about the initiative to dip into their own pockets. Those who did feel very strongly about it, unfortunately also were those who could not afford more than a pittance. I had written a hundred letters to people I knew and who, I thought might consider our efforts worthwhile. Only five replied in writing and signed up for a membership of R5 per month. There were negative reactions as well. An anonymous letter to the editor of a newspaper was entitled 'TUCSIN belongs to the lunatic fringe'. The style of this letter was similar to those previously addressed to me personally by my 'colleagues'.

Consequently the Rössing Foundation rented the entire property of the Remmer Clinic and we arranged an inaugural party for Literacy and English classes to be offered by the Rössing Foundation. One of the reactions to this occasion was a letter from a Windhoek Town Councilor warning me against "drumming up gatherings of blacks in the urban area" (samedromming van nie-blankes in die stedelike gebied).

My appointment as Principal to the Rössing Foundation Education Centre stabilised my financial situation and allowed for some creativity in changing the imbalances in the local society. Offering free adult education was an invaluable service to the majority of the population and I remained optimistic about there still being room for working on my priorities with regard to research and the promotion of higher academic education. This ambition was reflected by another gesture of the L.S.B. Leakey Foundation. Professor Ned Munger frequently visited South Africa. On one of his visits to Namibia he offered the newly established TUCSIN two postgraduate scholarships in archaeology at the California Institute of Technology.

This was announced by way of a press release. There were various enquiries about the conditions for taking up the scholarships, none of which could be met. This illustrated the shortcomings of the system of education, which was a favourite topic among the TUCSIN members. In the course of debating the viability of a university for Namibia it was pointed out that the first step would have to consist of preparing students for university. The pure sciences were the most neglected subjects in the 'black' schools. At the same time these were subjects vital for the development of the country, although TUCSIN never underestimated the importance of the arts. The chosen slogan was "…we cannot be independent unless we have our own scientists and artists…"

Robert Camby, a consulting engineer, who became deeply involved with TUCSIN, proclaimed this motto. His hobby was rock art and he was consumed by an interest in documenting the rock pictures of the Brandberg Mountain. On a three day climbing expedition up the Amis valley of that mountain massif we became utterly attracted to one another and embarked on a relationship that would last for almost two decades. Robert had been exploring the valleys of the Brandberg and had come across an area marked by innumerable stone cairns. Having photographed and mapped the sites he approached the State Museum and offered his help in undertaking further research. The response was a threat of being prosecuted should he be found doing any work of his own in the area. This matched a communication I had received from the South African Monuments Council denying me the right to do any more archaeological fieldwork involving excavations in the Namib Desert. This was a severe blow because I had the opportunity of joining a rock art research project in cooperation with Harald Pager. He was documenting the rock paintings in the Brandberg and the Deutsche ForschungsGesellschaft was funding archaeological research aimed at complementing his epoch making work.

The fraternity at the State Museum had given Harald a similarly hostile reception as Robert had received and of which I too, had been given a taste via anonymous letters. Harald Pager and his two assistants from the town of Uis would spend weeks at a time moving from one rock art site to the next high up in the Brandberg massif. Harald, a commercial artist fascinated by copying rock art, had become known for the beautiful books on paintings in the Drakensberg Mountains in South Africa. He was meticulously copying every painting onto fully annotated plastic sheets from which they could be reproduced into books. While he was working in the mountain massif his Land Rover would be parked at the foot of the Brandberg. At one point the archaeologist at the State Museum wrote him a letter maligning him on account of being unqualified to do the work that he was doing and threatening to set Harald's vehicle alight while he was working on the mountain. We tried to deal with these experiences as best we could by not allowing them to deter us from pursuing our goals. Harald was made to feel most welcome at TUCSIN. When his wife, Shirley moved from South Africa to join him in Namibia, TUCSIN House was her home for a while. Robert was incredibly resourceful and dynamic. In next to no time he had drawn up a constitution for TUCSIN and convinced two other founder members to contribute towards the deposit of a property in Windhoek's Main Street: TUCSIN HOUSE. It became a popular venue for socializing and meeting people who shared an interest in education, research, discovering more about our beloved country and getting to know one another. One project after the other was designed. Feasibility studies were written up for submission to the Board of TUCSIN comprising erudite members such as the late Dr Tjijorakisa, Anton Lubowski, Hans-Karl Ruegheimer and Dieter Aschenborn as well as other well-known Namibians Drs Hans Scholz and Zed Ngavirue, Joshua Hoebeb, Charly Hartung, Urbanus Dax , Browne Neels and many more.

The measures applied here were very similar to those we had experienced in the Kavango region. The privileged few who had been to the Kaokoveld had come back with wondrous tales about the scenic beauty of a landscape teeming with all kinds of wildlife and the exotic Himba-Herero. Rona MacCalman had also been to the area with Dr Steyn and had reported on Ovatjimba people using stone tools. The Ovatjimba were a sub-group of the Ovahimba.

In 1978 the first internal general elections were held in the country and a home-grown National Assembly was granted executive powers. Many of the restrictive policies of the South African Government were changed. Crossing the Red Line was no longer a big problem and I was keen to visit the area again, with time for activities other than distributing food. Robert enthusiastically shared my interests and we planned another trip to Kaokoland.

Robert and I were joined by Ismael Katjitae and Simeon Hamutenya, as TUCSIN students, John de Souza, a TUCSIN member from Swakopmund, Hans-Karl Ruegheimer and Claire Ritchie, an American Anthropologist working on a TUCSIN project in Bushmanland. We arranged to go back to the area to which we had taken relief supplies before.

By now I was pursuing so many different aims that it was hard to keep track of my motives. What did a trip to Kaokoland have to do with archaeology or with climatic change in the Namib? I remembered the conversation with Wade and Helge Laursen at Meob Bay about going to live with the allegedly stone-using Ovatjimba in Kaokoland. But let's face it, that was a poor excuse for going there on a one week trip. Curiosity and the excitement of the others looking forward to the experience infected me as well. The spirit we were promoting at TUCSIN was geared to exploring the country and to becoming acquainted with all sectors of Namibia's population. The concept of *Zeitgeist* occasionally crossed my mind. But there was literally no time to devote to such thoughts in an appropriate way.

The demands of our full-time jobs, which all of us were holding down, occasionally led to unwise decisions. One of them was to leave Windhoek after work on a Friday evening to meet up with Claire Ritchie and John de Souza from Swakopmund, early on Saturday morning in Outjo from where we would then depart towards Kaokoland. Soon after the five of us from Windhoek had left in Robert's old short wheel base Land Rover and in Hans Karl's VW Combi, the lights of the Land Rover started to give in. As we were driving and as darkness was setting in, their performance deteriorated. Robert and Simeon in the Land Rover were leading the two car procession, driving slowly and relying more on the headlights of Hans-Karl's microbus behind them, than on the dim light of the Land Rover. Seated in the Combi, the eyes of Hans-Karl, Ismael and myself were glued to the vehicle in front of us. Tension would increase when a car passed us or came towards us.

One of those inconsiderate drivers approaching us had obviously neglected to dim his extremely bright headlights. We were blinded and all I saw for a split second were the stoplights of the Land Rover disappearing next to the road. We had just crossed a culvert over a steep sided riverbank. Hans Karl slammed on the brakes and turned around. There, several metres below the level of the road, beneath the culvert, we saw the Land Rover lying on its roof. It took a few minutes, which felt like an eternity, before we discovered Robert lying unconscious next to the car. Simeon was getting up from what had probably been a short spell of unconsciousness. Robert had cuts on his face, but he was breathing. Ismael, the aspirant medical student, lifted his eyelids and laconically informed me:

"He is alive."

Without moving his spine I was cradling his head in my lap and directed Ismael to try and find the first aid kit. Simeon was running around, obviously disoriented. Hans-Karl, on the verge of hysteria, was trying to establish radio contact and managed to send out a May-day signal – this was before the era of cell phones.

In figuring out our location we realised that we were almost equidistant from Okahandja and Otjiwarongo. This meant that either way the closest hospital was approximately 90 kilometres away. A car on the way to Otjiwarongo stopped and promised to have an ambulance sent out as soon as possible. It arrived within two hours. Robert had regained consciousness or semi-consciousness and made a few very funny remarks about us creating such a fuss but having poor taste in music – referring to the too-ta-ta of the ambulance. The para-medics assured me that his back was not broken because he could move both his feet.

By Saturday morning Claire and John de Souza, who had been travelling from Swakopmund, had been informed about the accident and had driven to Otjiwarongo to meet us there. Simeon and Robert had been hospitalised. After a thorough examination the doctor recommended two days rest for Robert on account of concussion, before continuing with the expedition. Most sane people would probably have decided to abandon the entire trip after this start. But we definitely including Robert - were so fired up in anticipation of all the - exciting things we were going to see and do that we rejected sanity and pushed ahead, minus one car.

Two days was the minimum of time needed to sort out all the matters arising from this unfortunate intervention. The contents of the Land Rover, which had been spilled in the dry riverbed in which the car had landed, had to be collected and re-allocated to the other two cars. The short wheelbase Land Rover was taken to a garage in Outjo. A few dozen fresh eggs had been converted to scrambled eggs for breakfast at the Onduri Hotel, managed by my friend Hannelore in Outjo. All the expedition members had moved there to her good care. On the third day we moved on, a little worse for wear, but in good spirits.

At Orupembe we met the first group of Himba people.

Communication was greatly facilitated by Ismael who spoke Herero, although in a different dialect. Two themes dominated our lengthy conversations: The drought and the war. I felt almost ashamed to broach subjects like traditions in stone tool work. But our hosts were extremely polite and accommodating. A discussion relating to resources and available raw materials led to a demonstration of their skill in working metal. I had asked about the source of the beautiful metal beads, which were adorning their headgear and skin clothing.

"They want some wire," Ismael was translating.

The atmosphere was charged with urgency or impatience and when Hans Karl offered our wire braai fork, no one objected. The Himba man deftly removed one of the prongs on the fork and started beating the wire with a hammerstone on a stone anvil. Within a few minutes he had produced two beautiful metal beads by using stone tools!

We became particularly friendly with Kamasitu Katjipombo. He told us – via Ismael – about the unbearable conditions, which the war situation had created. Both the freedom fighters and the SADF (South African Defence Force) wanted to enlist the Himba as informers or spies. Both promised rewards backed up by terrible threats should the Himba

At Orupembe we met the first group of Ovahimba. Left to right: Hans Karl Rugheimer, Ismael Katjitae, Kamasitu Katjipombo and the author.

prove untrustworthy. There was constant tension and suspicions were arising among the group themselves. Therefore Kamasitu had decided to leave the group together with his wife, daughter and mother-in-law. He begged us to give them a ride to a waterhole to the west of Orupembe. We had come from that direction and were headed for the plateau east of Orupembe. But Hans-Karl felt that his Combi would not make it up the escarpment and it was agreed that he would stay at Orupembe until the rest of us returned in a few days time. Consequently it was arranged that we would take Kamasitu and family to where he wanted to go on our way back. Before we left, Kamasitu warned us not to move around at night and to look out for landmines!

So we carried on driven by zeal and curiosity, oblivious of danger. We found a pleasant camping spot on the plateau and decided to make it a base from where to venture during the day and return at night. Simeon was going to guard the camp while the rest of us left early in the morning to explore the area. Omuzondowombe was a large settlement with a few goat kraals and only one enclosure with very few cattle because of the drought. After respectable introductions by courtesy of Ismael, people wanted to know why we had come to this area. Possibly they suspected us of being linked to the SADF. We tried to deal with political issues as diplomatically as possible and may have gained some credibility. We told people about TUCSIN. We gave them brochures with pictures of our black, brown and white office bearers.

Education invariably was an issue about which we could talk at length. John and Robert were interested in buying ethnographic artefacts and this was to our advantage as well. Our interest in photographing and filming such activities as preparing cosmetics from ochre and butter and in recording the playing of the musical bow and the beating of drums furthermore helped to break the ice. John and Claire then decided to move on to another area and it was agreed that they would be back before sundown so that we could return to our camp before dark.

Rolls of film and tape cassettes were filled. The Polaroid camera worked non-stop. The first time that it occurred to me to have a drink of water, the sun was already quite far down in the west and it was not going to slow down. Where were John and Claire?
They will soon be here, we were reassuring ourselves. Sometimes distances seem shorter driving there than coming back. Or had something happened to them?
Should we start walking back to our camp?

No, our newly found friends said. That is too dangerous. 'They' are starting to move around. I did not even care to ask who 'they' were.
And then Claire approached in the last rays of the setting sun. On foot. John's car was stuck in the sand and he had stayed in the car. The battery was flat. Claire had miraculously found her way back to tell us what had happened and where the car was. Our last car! Via Ismael, Claire explained to our Omuzondowombe hosts where the car was and we were informed in no uncertain terms that it was out of the question to get anyone now to help push the car out of the sand. That would have to wait till morning, because now 'they' were starting to move around. It was also mentioned that lions and hyenas were moving around at night. John had neither food nor drink. The seat cover was the only thing that could serve as a blanket.

Robert thought that it might just be possible to move the vehicle with a trick and a bit of human power. We shared these thoughts with our hosts-by-default. They had Ismael tell us that we were completely mad to want to walk back to the car during the night. In spite of the protestations two men agreed to take us to the car. Claire was clearly in no state to walk back and stayed at the village while Ismael, Robert and myself blindly followed the two men in single file into the pitch-black night. They set an unbelievable pace, which left no time for even the slightest hesitation. I managed to sense rather than see Ismael in front of me and knew that Robert was behind me. Every now and again I strode into a branch or stumbled across some obstruction and learned very quickly to just move on. Hardly a word was spoken and, mercifully, I did not have any doubt about our guides going where we wanted to go. Every nerve, every sense, every muscle was focused on moving forward for about two hours. When we saw John and the car I felt like an arrow that had hit the bull's eye. He had the seat cover draped around his shoulders and was very pleased to see us.

The Himba immediately lit a little fire, which made me realise that it was very cold. The rear wheels of the car were stuck in deep sand. The sand had to be dug away and Robert's trick depended on ensuring that the wheel could spin freely. Then a long belt was strung around the rim to be jerked powerfully when the car was started with the last juice in the battery. Everybody was pushing, sadly to no avail. There was no alternative but to give John the oranges we had brought for him and to turn back. By now we had heard a hyena and a lion. The pace seemed to have become even faster. We were moving in the same order. One of the few things which were said on the way were by Robert:
"Lions usually go for the last one in such a row." I stopped for the fastest pee in my life and thus offered my place in the row to Robert. But he was too much of a gentleman to make use of the opportunity.

165

Back 'home' Claire was huddled next to a tiny fire together with four young women. She had been given two blankets with the understanding that they were for all of us. This resulted in a unique sleeping arrangement with the four of us lying like herrings on top of one blanket and underneath the other. Movements, like turning onto the side had to be done in unison or else Claire or Ismael would lose cover. As the temperature dropped even lower my head kept inching closer and closer to the fire, which consisted of only a few embers by the early morning hours.

The first light saw us collecting whatever we could find to put onto the remains of the fire and more or less grabbing at the first little flames flickering up. Gradually people were emerging from the huts. One group had been sitting around the fire all night. In the east the sky was turning red when we heard the engine of a car. It passed at some distance from the village. Within a few minutes we could hear another car approaching. This time it was John's Land Rover. An army car had hauled him out! What a relief! We thanked the people for their hospitality. I sensed that we did have a lot to be grateful for because it would have been understandable if they had considered it too dangerous to accomodate such an odd crowd.

Simeon also heaved an enormous sigh of relief when we returned to our camp. Back at Orupembe Hans-Karl had rested and was in good spirits. Kamasitu Katjipombo was waiting for us and we resumed our conversation about the use of stone or stone tools.

It was an interesting experience trying to find translations of concepts from the Himba dialect of the Herero language into English and/or Afrikaans, let alone German. We were talking about the natural appearance of a stone. I wanted to find out whether Kamasitu could or would distinguish a naturally shaped stone from one, which had been used or shaped by human hand. Ismael had just told me that according to Kamasitu there were about twenty different terms for different kinds of stone in his language.

We talked about stones

I had collected a few pieces of rock to refer to in our conversation. Several of them had characteristics, which I wanted to get identified because archaeologists had figured out that these were the crucial criteria ruling the production and use of stone artefacts.

Kamasitu picked up a stone which I would have called a natural or unworked stone with angular, unweathered facets and declared:

"This is a stone like God made it."

I thought this might imply the stone not having been eroded and picked up a smoothly, water worn cobble:

"And this one – is it any different?"

Answer: "God made all stones."

I: "But this one looks different, doesn't it?"

Kamasitu: "Yes, because it was lying in the water."

I felt like an idiot. But I didn't even know how to explain that feeling.

I picked up a quartz flake, which I had managed to remove from a larger stone and which was therefore showing a fresh cleavage, or 'flake scar with a point of percussion' in archaeological parlance.

"Do you think this stone is different from the others?"

"Yes, it is white – the others are brown."

Obviously I was on the wrong track.

Kamasitu Katjipombo

Another try: "Do you think stones are useful in the work you do every day?"

"Oh yes, we use them for building our houses and the women grind the red stones to make cream for the skin." All three of us were really sincerely trying to come up with the 'right' answers.

"But would you use a stone as a knife, for instance?" I was determined to get at Stone Age terminology! Kamasitu: " No, we have metal knives," he pulled out a pocketknife, "and there are also big knives and pangas." Me again:

"What about the olden days? Do you think people used stones before they had metal?"

"Perhaps. But that is very long ago. But, nowadays if we are out in the veld, we can also cut with stone. It can be very sharp."

Ha, I was getting somewhere! I picked up a weathered scraper I had been lucky enough to find along the road. According to a modern Stone Age technologist it could have been identified as a Middle Stone Age scraper or tortoise shell core – timewise at least 30 000 years ago. Probably my eyes were shining behind my sunglasses:

"Do you think this stone was made by a person?! Even a long time ago?"
Kamasitu picked up the Middle Stone Age scraper and examined it very carefully. Then, with conviction:
"No, this is a stone like God made it."
I was not going to give up. Turning to Ismael, I said:
" I would like to get at the concept of tradition, age, old habits. Can you try to explain that somehow?"
I was straining every nerve to follow with my pathetically limited Herero vocabulary what they were talking about, but 'huka' was all I could really identify. 'huka' means long ago. Finally Ismael turned to me and said:
" Kamasitu knows poems and songs from the old people. He would like to recite or to sing them to you."
I felt like jumping out of my skin. Forget the rocks and the stones. This was the real stuff. We had been struggling quite a while and it was getting dark. I suggested preparing some food and then we would get together after supper. It was a unique evening. After everyone had received a healthy helping of potjiekos, most of the group felt like retiring. I prepared some tea for Kamasitu, Ismael and myself and we settled down next to the fire. The tape recorder was on and the hours slipped by as Kamasitu briefly explained the context of each piece he was then singing or reciting. When I finally got into my sleeping bag it felt as though the dream was just continuing ...about majestic cattle which form the axis around which Himba culture rotates….

PRAISING CATTLE

They were there
There were oxen
With blazes
Which were ridden by the son of Kakove of Muundjua
The oxen of Mbiringindji
Of the daughter of Tjingombemundu
Of the sister of the father of Nehambo
The red one with the long flank
They were there
The oxen of Mberovandu
They were there
The huge oxen of Tjimbembe of Ngahamuani's daughter
The red one with iron and steel horn
They were there
The oxen of the Mbongora clan
Of Tjikuambi's son, the mongoose
Which dug a grave
Of Handji of mopani worms the spotted belly
They were there
Those belonging to the person of Kazenguaza
Of the Maorongo tree
The cream coloured mongoose
Bit the chief underneath his apron
They were there
The morning rester with the big chest
They were there

OMUTANDU

Omu za ri, mwa ri nozongombe
Ozonduwombe zongongouara ondanga
Nda kavirw'omunaa Kakove kaMuundjua

Ozonduwombe, omu za ri zooMbirigindji
Yomusuko waTjingombemundu
Tjomutena wa hi yaNehambo
Indjiokaserandu konusu omuroro
Omu za ri ozonduwombe
zooMberovandu mbena
Omu za ri ozonduwombe
Yamusuko waTjimbembe tjaNgahamuani

Indji okaserandu konya yotjivera
Omu za ri ozonduwombe zombongora

zomuzandu waTjikuambi ing omukundakunda
mbwa sombira
Omu za ri mona mo nohandji
tjomungu ondamberova otjoruwowo
Omu za ri zomundu waKazenguava komuti
Omukuambi waMaorongo, orupuka ururumbu
ndwa rumata omuhona kehi yozohira

Omu za ri nosuvamuhuka indji okotjitjari

Omu za ri nohandji yomitamba

168

English	Otjiherero
Even Handji of the valleys	
The bull of Kapiriona*	Ondwezu yaKapiriona
They were there	Omu za ri nomburi otjeanga
Even the buffalo with the dewlap	
The bitter like poison·	
They were there	Omu za ri mona musi
Even one of the twins	
They were there	Omu za ri nombahona
Even the zebra coloured with round hoofs	Omu za ri nombandaoro yotjikoti onguma
The male	
They were there	Omu za ri nokaserandu kondjerera
Even the red one with the light patch	
They were there	Omu za ri notjihupuro
The spade*'	ozondwezu nondawa yamusuko waNangenda
They were there	
Even the nondawa*" coloured one of Nangenda's daughter ·	
They were there	Omu za ri nondamberamatundu indji oketjengo
Even the chaser of homesteads*''' with the big penis	
They were there	Omu za ri ozondwezu noya Kapiriona
The bulls – even Kapiriona's	
The one which banishes the rain	Indji onganda yombura
They were moving around	za ri mokati kovirongo
And they were drinking out of these wells	aze nu mozondjombo nda
They were there	Omu za ri ozondwezu nokaserandu
The bulls – even the red one	
Which prefers the 'nduma' grass	ku ka pomb'onduma
The one which likes the fleshy seeds	ku ka suvera otjihipiro
The one which likes the fibrous flesh	ku ka suvera onyama yozosepa
They were there	
There was the bull of Pahere's mother	Omu za ri mwa ri ondwezu yanaaPahere
The one with the spot on its tail	ondjo kotjinganda
There was the black thighed of the daughter	mwa ri ombinde yomukazona okenena
The gigantic ones	ozongutirwa omu za ri
They were there	Omu za ri nongande
Even the one from Ngarere's village	yongarererendjindjo komutjira
With bushy tail…	otjazenga

*Kapiriona – name of a cow; *' spade – metaphor for an ox; *" nondawa – a special colour;
*'''chasing cattle from the homesteads – refers to a traditional race.

Wife and daughter of Kamasitu Katjipombo

Early the next morning we packed and with Kamasitu and his family on board we left for the waterhole where Kamasitu wanted to be dropped off. I wrestled with the idea of leaving a man and his wife, with the blind old mother and adolescent daughter at a waterhole on a barren plain on the edge of the desert. Two hessian bags contained their belongings. We gave them every scrap of food we had left and tried to convince ourselves that they had a chance of surviving.

Back in our other world there was news, mail and lots of work waiting for us. Jerry Tobias had managed the Education Centre extremely well. More and more people wanted to take classes in English and Literacy and the Rössing bosses were talking about building a new, large centre in another part of town. I was excited about this and enthusiastically joined in conceptualising a relevant design. I would have loved to also accommodate TUCSIN in these plans but that was not possible.

In my personal mail I found an invitation to deliver a lecture on the Archaeology of Namibia to the Afrika Society of Switzerland. When I told Jürgen Richter, a German student of archaeology, who had been referred to TUCSIN by one of our members about this, he offered to arrange a presentation at his university in Erlangen as well.

His friend, Cornelia Limpricht, did the same for me at her university in Cologne. These contacts developed into solid friendships and Cornelia has been the official representative of TUCSIN in Europe ever since. Her first assignment consisted of arranging appointments with V.I.Ps for me during my visit to Switzerland and Germany in February 1983. The results of that trip had far-reaching consequences for TUCSIN.

The cordial relationship with my hosts in Switzerland would lead to continued cooperation

170

in terms of publications and in library and museum work. In Germany I learned an enormous amount about how the German Government and its politics worked. By following the excellent timetable of appointments Cornelia had made, and continued to make in accordance with the meetings I was having, I ended up initiating several significant deals for TUCSIN.

The Konrad Adenauer Stiftung (KAS) agreed to fund a course in which 25 Namibians would be prepared for university study in the natural science fields. They would also consider applications by the graduates of the TUCSIN Complementary Course for scholarships to South African Technical Colleges. The Deutsche Welt Hunger-Hilfe (DWHH) agreed to support two development projects we had proposed: setting up a cooperative for women making clothes and initiating a project aimed at preventing further desertification in East Hereroland.

The Deutscher Akademischer AustauschDienst (DAAD) agreed to provide scholarships for a number of Namibian students at South African universities and six students were to be accommodated at German universities, provided they could satisfy the entrance requirements. These two concessions were hard won in the course of lengthy discussions with officials in the organization and in Government departments. The record of African students at German universities had not been good. Often they could not meet the necessary academic requirements and had problems getting used to the German environment. I was told dreadful stories about students suffering from mental disorders as a result of homesickness and even committing or attempting suicide. Paradoxically, students who were refusing to return to their home countries after completion of their studies, presented the other problem.

By the time I returned to Namibia, Ismael had left for studies in South Africa and was reporting on a daily basis about one bad thing after the other that was happening to him there. The parliamentary consent allowing him to study at the 'white' university was not given. I told him about the arrangement with the DAAD and we decided to try to get him enrolled at a German university.

When I fetched him from the airport on his return from Johannesburg I could not help thinking about some of the stories they had told me at the DAAD about students not being able to cope with the conditions they found themselves in. The tall young man was huddling in the seat of the car as though he was trying to withdraw into himself.
"I want to tell you something," he said, looking at me sideways.
"If I had not met you people at TUCSIN I would now hate all white people, after the experiences I have had."

Before it was possible to engage full-time personnel to work at TUCSIN, members would meet for lunch at the Thueringer Hof Hotel every Tuesday. It was allowed to bring visitors and usually a vivacious group would assemble around the big round corner table with the sign 'Reserved for Mrs Tucsin'. The week after Ismael's return, Robert Camby brought Professor Müller as a guest. He was the President of the University of Saarbruecken in Germany and his visit seemed ordained. He was introduced to Ismael and was obviously impressed by him. When I told him about my meeting with the DAAD the deal was clinched. The University of Saarbrücken accepted Ismael Katjitae into their Faculty of Medicine. It was the start of a long and fruitful cooperation.

Three more students went to the University of Saarbruecken. They all had a second home wherever Cornelia Limpricht was, a fact, which contributed significantly to the success in their studies. Jerry Tobias and others obtained a scholarship to study in England. Joseph Diescho, Clifford Olivier and Issy Namaseb qualified for Fulbright scholarships to go to USA. But there were many more students who, we thought had the potential to embark on university careers, but who did not satisfy the entrance requirements of good universities. This led us to design a course to upgrade skills of students in the most neglected subjects, that is the science subjects and the English language. The Konrad Adenauer Stiftung funded this Complementary Course for ten years. It proved highly successful and became a hallmark of TUCSIN.

The issue of a university for Namibia was debated seriously. We came to the conclusion that our numerically small population could realistically expect to have our academic 'winners' gain internationally recognised qualifications at the best universities world-wide. In return Namibia could contribute globally by becoming a centre of excellence in specialised fields such as arid lands studies, African history, anthropology and/or archaeology. We were confident that good research and teaching in one or two of the specialised fields mentioned would attract local talent and interest as well as international attention.

In my 1978 report on a study trip to Europe I had written about the young field of Palaeo-ethno-botany, which is the European term for what I called archaeo-botany. An international organisation for Palaeo-ethno-botany had been established in 1975 but there had not yet been any members working in Africa. The aims of this young field were to reconstruct environments of the past, to examine the spread of different plants, particularly food plants and to augment ethnological information. Would this not have been a marvellous niche to fill for a University of Namibia? We could have adjusted the aims to include the spread of animals, particularly domestic animals. Furthermore we could have decided to concentrate on arid lands and we would have had an excellent profile. Such an approach would have used our unique conditions for the sake of qualifying Namibia as a singular venue for specialised studies. The work would be of interest to arid areas covering seven per cent of the world's land surface.

This work would also enrich the field of basic education. In my mind I saw textbooks for subjects like 'Environment Studies', 'Development Studies' or 'Natural Economy' becoming popular. What would be more stimulating than to be on the forefront of knowledge about our own highly specialised surroundings? The envisaged curriculum would promote the development of skills relevant to the economy of Namibia. In that way basic education could provide learners with skills to earn them a living. The same basic qualification should also be useful for those who wanted to continue with higher academic education. It should be recognised by tertiary institutions inside as well as outside the country.

The Complementary Course represented the first step ensuring that Namibians interested in higher academic education would qualify for the best institutions of tertiary study anywhere. Many of the Complementary Course students went to universities and colleges in the United States, Canada, Australia, Europe and South Africa. As a further step at university level in Namibia we would like to have planned basic courses for the most common professions in the country. Teachers, technicians and personnel in the building construction and farming should be able to qualify as professionals in their vocations. Again, this qualification which would have been tailored to Namibian needs, should also be accredited at other universities.

As we were forging ahead implementing one project after the other we were also exposed to rumours and threats. One rumour had it that the success TUCSIN was having with getting Namibians enrolled at universities all over the world, stimulated the establishment of the Academy. This institution was modelled on the South African bush colleges with a comprehensive administrative structure. The academic staff was imported from South Africa. The relationship to TUCSIN was strained, although there were individuals who cooperated with us. Another element of the delicate situation consisted of veiled or direct threats we received. One of them consisted of an official letter informing us that it was illegal to use the word 'university' as part of TUCSIN's name. One of our Board members, Joshua Hoebeb, who later became the ambassador to South Africa and Botswana, was shot at when he left TUCSIN House after a meeting there. The next day we also found marks of bullets on the boundary wall of TUCSIN and a hole in one of the window pains.

The Board of TUCSIN decided on a policy of keeping a low profile. We tried to ignore all negative events and would approach the media only if we had some success to report such as students being awarded scholarships or the visits of scientists who would offer talks at TUCSIN House. One of our visitors from the University in Münster became intrigued by our ideas of a university for Namibia. He went as far as inviting us in 1985 together with representatives of the Academy and the United Nations Institute for Namibia (UNIN) in Lusaka to a round table discussion about a future university for Namibia. Sadly the representatives of UNIN could not make it to Münster.

TUCSIN facilitated the establishment of the Yvonne Steyn School at Naos, the farm of Board member Dr Hans Scholz. Similarly TUCSIN was instrumental in founding a school for the Topnaar at Utuseb along the Kuiseb River.

Topnaar Hoofman Kootjie meets A.G. Steyn to discuss the establishment of a school at Utuseb

The first hostel in the background as provided by the Topnaar community

The official openings of these two schools received modest publicity. Work on the Rehoboth Library was progressing well by way of receiving donations of books and by getting the Rehoboth Government to make premises available. Two rooms adjacent to the Town Hall housed the first books of the Rehoboth Library. The official inauguration took place only two years after the library had started operating. The guest of honour at this auspicious occasion was the well-known South African philosopher and writer, Adam Small. The event was a community celebration. Coming from Windhoek by car our guest was welcomed by a cavalcade of horses linking up with an army of drum majorettes leading him to the Town Hall where the official inauguration was to take place. An inscribed plaque of pink marble from Witvlei had been affixed to the wall next to the entrance of the two rooms comprising the library. The event was furthermore marked by the inaugural performance of the play "Krismis vir Map Jacobs" which had recently been written by Adam Small.

I was anxious about people not coming to the play and imagined only two rows of seats being taken up in the huge Town Hall. What a delightful surprise to have the hall crammed with men, women and children of all sizes and ages! After the first act a tiny tot in nappies crossed the aisle in front of the stage and promptly lost some solid waste. Adam Small's wife Rosi, was delighted and exclaimed that it was the best omen for a first performance.

Ms Yvonne Steyn plants the first tree at the Utuseb School in 1978

CHAPTER 12

THE REHOBOTH MUSEUM

Soon after 'our' (first public) library had started operating, the Kapteinsraad had approached Robert Camby to suggest the establishment of another institution which would benefit the Rehoboth Community. Robert's idea of a museum was warmly welcomed. It turned out that it was something, which had been talked about ten years earlier during the Rehoboth Baster centenary in 1970. I felt compelled to inform the Kapteinsraad about my standing with the government and the South African Monuments Council who had withdrawn my work permit. Kaptein Diergaardt's reaction was a great relief. Since the Rehoboth Gebiet was used by the South African government as a model for separate development it meant that the South African laws would have to be promulgated by the Kapteinsraad before they were applicable in their area of jurisdiction. The Kapteinsraad had not promulgated the Monuments Act of 1969 and were thus free to recognise me as they saw fit.

As in the case of the library, TUCSIN was assigned the task of producing a feasibility study. Obviously the plans for the museum related well to the aims of TUCSIN. The museum could function as an appropriate link between higher academic learning and the community at the grass roots level. The seed was sown for a symbiotic relationship between TUCSIN and the Rehoboth Museum. Cliff Olivier, a High School teacher in Rehoboth was one of the first students to be awarded a Fulbright scholarship entitling him to obtain a Master's degree in Science Teaching. Many youngsters from Rehoboth, today qualified as teachers, lawyers and medical doctors, were to follow.

In 1985 the first ever Rehoboth Museum seminar was offered and became an annual event. A Steering Committee was established and interested members of the community were treated to talks, demonstrations and fieldwork experiences of a high standard. The stone tuyère site at which I had worked twelve years previously provided an excellent field laboratory for demonstrating the importance of responsible collection and documentation of archaeological data. It also provided an introduction into the prehistory of the area. One of the excursions to rock art sites in the Rehoboth area served to demonstrate the tracing and copying of rock engravings.

The first seminars lasted for several days and took place even before the Rehoboth Government had made premises available to the museum. The beautifully appointed Reho-

The late Willi Metzler and Anzel Bayer tracing a rock engraving in the Rehoboth area

Spa had just been completed and provided a wonderful venue and accommodation for visitors, who were becoming a regular feature of the museum's work. Although the socio-political conditions were fast changing during the early 1980's, outsiders still were an anomaly in the non-white town, which was the second largest urban settlement in Namibia at the time.

Volunteers renovated the residence of the first Postmaster

When the Kapteinsraad had allocated a plot right next to the Post Office to be used for the museum we spent a long string of weekends renovating the dilapidated historical building, which had been the residence of Rehoboth's first Postmaster almost a hundred years before.

The Steering Committee was planning for the future. Work at the museum was to concentrate on three specific areas of interest. The aim was to educate the local community, in particular the school children, about the conservation of the natural environment, about the history of the Baster people as well as about the prehistory of the area documented by sites with ancient stone tools, rock art and evidence of metalwork three hundred years ago. In later years Contemporary Art was added as a fourth area of specialisation to this budding institution of higher learning. Two special workshops for artists provided the beginning of a sculpture park at the Rehoboth Museum. Andrew van Wyk, a well known artist at home in Rehoboth, offered the first formal art classes to local children at the museum. This was a great success culminating in a special exhibition in Windhoek's Kleine Gallerie. A few years later Andrew van Wyk opened an art school in Rehoboth.

The physical infrastructure of the museum needed to be expanded. We needed more space and requested an enlargement of the yard. The Kapteinsraad also granted us this wish and we started the museum's ethno-botany programme by planting indigenous trees all along the border of the enlarged museum grounds. But we also wanted more buildings. Imagination, expertise, enthusiasm, an enormous amount of hard work plus a lot of money were needed to realise our dreams. We seemed to have fair supplies of all the vital commodities except for money. Robert Camby in his position as consulting engineer could organise many services to be provided through the government and our enthusiasm, which encompassed sweeping the floors, sanding the wood work, writing up proposals, leading meetings and doing public relations work, seemed to be contagious. We did, however, overestimate our capacity.

I realised this very clearly when Robert had a heart attack in 1985. Fortunately he recovered very well, but I knew that the Rehoboth Museum could not operate successfully unless we had full time personnel. On another tour of conferences in Great Britain, Germany and in the USA I was on the lookout for money and help. A contact with an organisation called Project Trust in Britain and a proposal for funds to the German government almost miraculously provided access to both these resources.

In looking at my daily agenda it was obvious that the RFEC (Rössing Foundation Education Centre) was the most expendable item in terms of needing my skills and talents. The newly built centre on the boundary of central Windhoek and Khomasdal had turned out beautifully. I had even managed to install a library, although the first request to the Foundation had been countered with the words: "…But we thought the idea of the centre was to provide teaching…" When I lightheartedly related this to a prominent visitor – a representative of the USA – the request was reconsidered and a truly lovely library was designed and built. All the centre now needed was sound administration of courses in literacy training, Basic English, needlework, office procedure, basic mechanics, arts and crafts. There had been requests by the public for offering such courses. When we could find suitable qualified teachers the Board of the Rössing Foundation would decide on offering courses according to suggested curricula. With the Foundation up and running the Rössing Uranium Management had appointed a Director. I suspected that one of his important tasks was to ensure that I would not contaminate the work of the Foundation with TUCSIN's

The Administrative Officers of the newly built Rössing Foundation Education Centre

ideals and principles. The Rössing Foundation was bent on supplying a little education to as many Namibians as possible as cost effectively as possible. One of the mine's Public Relations Officers had once asked me in which way the image of the mine could best be promoted in Namibia. I had replied that desalination of seawater would be the most worthy and notable contribution to the development of the country. This, however, was considered to be too expensive an option. Consequently the decision was taken to invest in education as the next most useful way of gaining acceptance if not popularity with the government of Namibia then and after Independence. TUCSIN's philosophy of offering the youth with good academic potential the best possible education did not fit into the mine's policy. Appointing me to establish the Foundation did make good use of my entrepreneurial skills and was convenient in distracting me from issues about the sustainability of providing fossil water from the underground aquifers of the dry riverbeds in Namibia for the washing of uranium.

Against this background the Director of the Foundation and the Rössing Management were happy to offer me a gold plated handshake after nine years of cooperation. The package enabled me to do a survey of archaeological sites in the Rehoboth area as well as further work on the unique method of prehistoric copper smelting. With more time at my disposal I could also deal with TUCSIN projects, which were demanding attention and administration. The Complementary Course, generously funded by the Konrad Adenauer Stiftung was now enrolling 25 students every year. A shorter version of the course, called the TUCSIN ENRICHMENT PROGRAMME (TEP) was offered at the Rehoboth Museum as well as to schools in rural areas. Scholarships were awarded to increasing numbers of students every year. More and more visiting scientists and students were rubbing shoulders with TUCSIN members and students. Excursions to the budding Rehoboth Museum were a constant item on programmes and itineraries.

My most ardent desire to devote myself to more research on reconstructing past climates by developing the field of archaeo-botany, or by finding out more about early metal working, provided no possibility of generating an income. On the contrary it required capital for equipment and basic facilities as well as money for running expenses. In discussing these matters, both Robert and I felt that the museum could develop to include a research facility. It would be an invaluable educational resource, not only for Rehoboth, but for the country and the region as a whole.

I saw a museum in collaboration with a library as contributing to the quality of life for the community in Rehoboth. There were those two hundred teachers, about whom we had talked at Hennops Cave and at least as many civil servants in the well functioning administrative centre, which Rehoboth was at the time. The two institutions could offer stimulation and entertainment in a town where these concepts were limited to discos, bars and shebeens.

Ethno-botany was obviously linked to my interest in archaeo-botany and I was aware of the local knowledge about indigenous plants, which had not yet been recorded in writing. The public was encouraged to bring in any indigenous plant, which served some or other economic or social purpose. The first reaction to this request resulted in Hilde Dentlinger bringing me the 'veld aartappel' or //haba. I was busy cleaning up one of the rooms, which had just been painted in 'our' museum when she offered me this unfamiliar brown potato as a 'speciality'. It was warm and she had a blob of butter and some salt wrapped in a piece of paper. I tasted. I liked it – and had another one. Then I gave some more to Robert. He said they reminded him of truffles. Indeed these were Kalahari truffles (*Terfezia pheilii*) – counterparts of that European delicacy, which no ordinary person like us would have been able to afford over there. This 'discovery' took some time to really penetrate and then there was a great deal of talk about the financial implications this might have. A year later we heard that there were farmers in the Kalahari who already had a lucrative truffle scheme going with contacts in Germany.

The next exciting 'discovery' was the 'gamaku' or Devil's Claw *(Harpago)* – which was being marketed for its medicinal value in Europe and locally. It also occurs in the Rehoboth area and faces the threat of becoming extinct in Botswana. These issues related well to the concern about preserving the natural environment. People started bringing in plants and we would record the information that accompanied them. The most salient facts would be put on labels or plaques attached to the plants. As a next step Information Sheets were designed where the information we had collected and compared with known records was presented more elaborately. These Information Sheets turned out to be one form of publishing the information which the museum was collecting. Gradually Information Sheets were produced to accompany every exhibit of the museum. Ultimately a loose- leaf file resembling a book was envisaged. It targeted the school population of Rehoboth - and the rest of the world, for that matter.

The contact with Project Trust in Britain came to fruition in 1986. Angela Davis and Jane Birchenough were expected to arrive in Namibia after they had completed their A-levels at an English High School. They were prepared to work for their living at the Rehoboth Museum for one whole year. Their first introduction to Rehoboth consisted of getting to know Kaptein Hans Diergaardt over a cup of tea at our home in Windhoek. He gave the rather formal meeting a delightful turn when he said in heavily accented English:

"You will cause a revolution in Rehoboth." And after a short hesitation:
"But it will be a nice revolution."

Indeed, Angela and Jane and their 14 successors over a period of eight years did cause more than a stir in the community. I give them full credit for having been instrumental in establishing the Rehoboth Museum as an invaluable educational institution and research facility. The Project Trust volunteers were highly intelligent, utterly dedicated, mature and tough young women. It was a sheer pleasure working with them and observing how vast numbers of school children started coming to the museum where they had fun learning, where they discovered their own capabilities and the excitement of simply using their senses in recognizing and identifying their own amazing environment. The girls also attracted young adults, yes, in particular young men, but also the older members of the community were inspired by the institution which was the first of its kind in a non-white community in the region.

Apart from developing a daily work routine at the museum, Angela and Jane also doubled up as fieldwork assistants while I was doing the survey of archaeological sites in the Rehoboth area. Dr Ernst Scherz' documentation of rock art sites served as a guide and occasionally we could add sites which had not yet been recorded in book form. Hilde Dentlinger, a mine of information on all aspects of the natural environment, was one of several local members of the museum who accompanied us on these exploratory excursions. Apart from obtaining a record of as many archaeological sites as possible I was looking for an Iron Age site which would be suitable for excavation.

The search for an Iron Age site represented a return to the theme that had stimulated my research in Malawi and that I had taken up at the State Museum. I had not forgotten about this while I was working on the reconstruction of past climates. The ensuing discoveries of how people in the central Namib had been living in the past linked up with the theme of documenting the development of economies on the threshold of the twentieth century in Namibia. Finds of pottery and early sheep herding related to the questions of developments leading from the Stone Age to the Iron Age. Clearly, the stone tuyères were a central issue.

Although I was no longer obliged to answer the questions: what am I trying to do? Why am I doing what I am doing? in front of a panel of professors I found that these questions were therapeutic. Choices and circumstances determined what I was doing. I had chosen to leave the State Museum and the University of the Western Cape. The fact that the South African Monuments Council had withdrawn my permit to continue with archaeological work in the Namib was another factor making work in Rehoboth attractive.

I was moving along on the basis of a few principles which could be identified as common denominators in whatever I was doing. The elements of curiosity and the fun of imagining scenarios were strong. Coupled to that was the desire to be in touch with reality. My faith in believing that knowledge was power. Did I want power? Yes, I wanted the power of deciding how to spend my time and what to do with my talents. I wanted the power of choosing the company I kept. To me that was the essence of the quality of one's life. I also wanted other people to have those powers. I hated the idea of oppression - of people being forced to do things they did not want to do. The puzzling question was how many other people felt the way I did?

The Steering Committee established a Board of Curators of the Rehoboth Museum which operated according to a constitution. The aims were clearly outlined. The policy of the Rehoboth Museum related to the need of people to gain or regain their self-respect. This would be promoted by discovering the history of people who had been indoctrinated by the idea that Africa had no history. The idea in itself cried out for correction. So I would gradually continue to motivate myself and continue with what I was doing.

The Rössing Foundation had funded an aerial survey of Rehoboth and its vicinity. This was an important aspect of my reconnaissance work. Helen Powell and Tamsin Collis, two Project Trust volunteers, who came to the museum in 1987/8, were part of this exercise. A helicopter labeled REHOBOTH MUSEUM provided an excellent advertisement for the museum.

This spin-off was reflected in a drastic increase of visitors to the museum. In the helicopter we followed the course of the Oanob River and its canyon, where a large dam was being constructed. Numerous sites dotted either side of the narrow river valley. They were marked by different kinds of stone arrangements ranging from stone circles of different sizes, stone cairns of different shapes and dung patches representing kraals where stock had been kept, to ruins of more modern and not so modern structures. These observations represented a store of information waiting to be recorded and studied. A stone ruin site deep in the canyon was particularly fascinating on account of its curved walls and un-western design.

We surveyed the area around Rehoboth for archaeological sites from a helicopter

It reminded me of similarly abandoned structures I had noticed in the Naukluft Massif: another complex of prehistoric data waiting for analysis.

In the course of following up the aerial survey on the ground I decided to excavate a number of stone cairns in the vicinity of the Drierivier smelting site excavated in 1970. This decision led to valuable information dating to the times of early copper smelting at Drierivier. The excavation of the first stone cairn was preceded by an exercise, which Robert Camby had suggested to ascertain at what depth below the surface we were likely to come across a find – whatever that might be. He used the principle of resistivity in the soil. Electricians use this Wenner method, which is internationally standardised, when they want to install underground cables and need to ensure that they do not collide with, for example, water pipes previously laid down.

An interesting ruin in the Oanob River canyon

A grid of one metre squares was measured out over an area with two stone arrangements similar in shape but of different size. A transect of measurements indicated that there was a change in compaction of the soil beneath both the stone cairns at a depth of about two metres. We started carefully dismantling the larger of the two cairns after every stone that could be seen from the surface had been marked with a number and had been plotted on graph paper.

Helga Kohl, friend and well-known photographer, documented the process on camera. The core team of excavators consisted of Helen Powell, Tamsin Collis, the two Project Trust volunteers, Robert, myself and occasional auxiliaries in the form of TUCSIN students and friends of the museum who were curious.

Members of the Drotski family who were living in the homestead a few kilometres east of the site would also drop by on their way to or from town every couple of days to see whether we were finding anything. We had talked to them about the significance or meaning of these stone arrangements, which were of no particular interest to them. They had dismissed them as 'ou boesman grafte' (old Bushman graves). Once the large stones lying above the natural surface of the ground had been removed, the stone slabs were concentrated on a smaller area in an otherwise homogeneous sandy deposit. I had identified this layer as a river terrace at a level of one to two metres above and a few hundred metres south of the present riverbed.

Tamsin Collis, Helga Kohl and the author plotting the stones at the Drierivier grave site - Dicka and Cassandra for security in the shade of the camping table

The excitement which accompanies the beginning of an excavation tends to subside as a daily routine of plain hard work sets in. This also happened at the Drierivier Cairn 1 excavation. Robert had to get back to his office in Windhoek during the week and that left Tamsin Collis, Helen Powell and me slogging on our own most of the time. The girls were staying in a small teachers' apartment in one of the school hostels in Rehoboth. I was occupying a bungalow in the lovely new Spa together with Dicka and Cassandra, my mother's two dackels (dachshound), which were in my care at the time. At crack of dawn I would pick up the girls and all of us would pile into my not so new, but comfortable Mercedes to drive the 15 kilometres to the excavation site.

It was the month of February when the normal temperatures of approximately 38° C were exacerbated by humidity – something that is rather abnormal in this arid region. So we were treated to excruciating heat increasing with every centimetre with which we dropped the level of the excavation. After a few days we had narrowed our work down to four square metres covering the center of the larger stone cairn.

A few days were marked by cool weather and by drizzle, which led to another extraordinary situation: We were longing for a hot cup of tea. For this we had to light a little fire under the protection of an umbrella! After tea we got back into the car and spent an hour reading until the sky cleared before we returned to the work of recording and then removing the stones. It looked as though a number of stones had been put into a hole in the ground before a large cairn was built up on the surface.

Plant remains looking like wood or large roots were found amongst the quartzite slabs at the top of the conical cairn. We speculated that a tree or bush might have grown – or was it planted? – on top of the pile of stones. We arbitrarily identified layers of the stones we lifted and gave all of them different names, including those of Dicka and Cassandra, in case we might be required to rebuild this construction one day.

Until we reached a depth of one metre below the natural surface nothing particularly unusual or interesting was found apart from several white quartz cobbles. They seemed to have been strewn amongst the dark coloured slabs of quartzite. On closer inspection a few of them looked like the proverbial chopper tools of Early Stone Age times, dating back two million years or more. Although I recorded this observation in a few rough sketches I dismissed the idea of any implication this might have conjured up about the age of this stone arrangement. During later reconnaissance work I discovered a widespread layer of pebbles and cobbles which dates to a phase in the history of the river long before the time of the graves and the metal working site.

At a depth of 1,25 metre below the natural surface Tamsin brushed open a bone fragment. It was not moved while we carefully brushed around it to see whether there was more bone in the vicinity. But there wasn't. Instead we uncovered a perfect circle of seven stones arranged around the bone fragment in the dead centre. It looked like the head of a femur. The local medical Doctor identified it as being human! After removing more loose ground we saw that there was a flat stone lying right beneath the piece of bone. Having run out of our own names we called this level the PIT.

Beneath the PIT we dug through a layer of sand, which seemed less well compacted than the surrounding deposit. I did not dare voice my speculation that this might indicate the grave shaft because we were once more facing the situation of having to extend the excavation. The two square metre trench was becoming too deep to get into and out of. We needed a step, implying that an adjacent square had to be excavated. It could be done a little faster than we had been going so far. But it still meant several hours of physical work because we could not yet throw care to the wind. Definite proof of this being a 'simple' grave was not yet at hand.

Luckily it was weekend time and visitors again were starting to arrive. They were immediately put to work and by Sunday morning we could once more proceed with extending the excavation below the PIT. We hit another layer of flat stone slabs and beneath it another layer of pure sand covering yet more slabs of quartzite rock. At last at a depth of 1,90 metre below the surface some bone appeared. Gradually a well-preserved human skull came to light. It was part of a complete skeleton lying on its side on a bed of more stone slabs. The quartzite slabs had been arranged to enclose the skeleton in such a way that they resembled a stone sarcophagus.

DRIERIVIER CAIRN 2, TREE CAIRN SITE AND BOORGAT

Similar excavations were undertaken at twelve more sites in the vicinity of the copper-smelting site at Drierivier. Graves were found beneath only seven of these stone arrangements. Every effort at coming up with a theory failed as to which stone cairn represented a grave and which did not. The sample with which we were working was very small and I came to the conclusion that it would take many more excavations and a more discerning analysis to figure out the meanings of different stone cairns. Stones have always been around and were widely used in prehistoric times. It is more than likely that they were put to many different uses and that stone cairns meant different things at different times to different people.

My colleague Professor Alan Morris and a team of his students at the University of Cape Town helped with excavations at Drierivier 2, the smaller one of the two cairns to which we had applied the Wenner method of resistivity, the Tree Cairn site, (because it was found beneath an old camel-thorn tree), and the excavations of four graves at Boorgat (the name of the farm on which four cairns were found). The results provided a glimpse into the life of people living in the Rehoboth area two to three hundred years ago.

At Drierivier cairn 2 we found an object amongst the bones of the skeleton which was identified as a calcified hydatid cyst, which is known to develop in the human body. It encapsulates the embryo of a tapeworm to which sheep are the intermediate host. Dogs are the regular hosts of this parasite. The eggs of the tapeworm are passed through the dog's alimentary canal and thus land on grass, which gets eaten by sheep. The egg hatches in the body of the sheep and lodges in its organs such as the liver, which in turn is eaten by people. The human body reacts by enveloping the hatched egg in calcium. Such a growth is not in itself a cause of death, but complications could arise if this hard cyst presses on other organs, particularly if it is as large as the one we found. The significance of this discovery for prehistory is that it tells us that the people living here two to three hundred years ago had sheep and dogs.

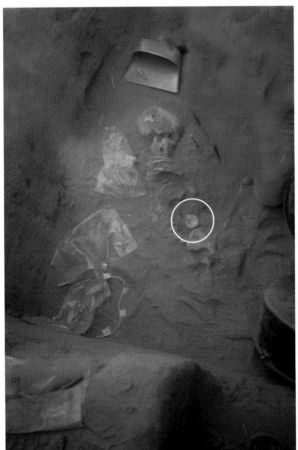

In his study of the Drierivier cairn 1 skeleton, Alan Morris noticed a particularly well-developed bone structure for the attachment of thigh muscles. This phenomenon has been observed in the bones of people who did a lot of horseback riding. The same could apply to the riding of donkeys or of oxen that were used as draught animals in southern Africa.

At the Tree Cairn site we found fragments of bone which were identified as belonging to cattle. Consequently a picture emerges in which the man who was buried beneath Drierivier Cairn 1 may have been riding an ox while the young woman buried next to him may have been looking after a herd of sheep with a dog or two.

Glass beads were found in the graves at Boorgat. How did the people living here two to three hundred years ago manage to get hold of beads which at that time were only known to have been made in India and/or in Europe? No doubt

A white hard object – a calcified hydatid cyst – was found amongst the bones of the skeleton of a young woman at Drierivier

there were trade routes in the sub-continent and from time to time people came into contact with each other. Beads would have been an item well suited to trading and bartering. This therefore provided yet another dimension in our perception of how the prehistoric inhabitants of the Rehoboth area were operating.

Dr Duncan Miller of the University of Cape Town was the kind of specialist whom I had hoped to meet since the work at the Drierivier smelting site in 1970/1. Previously I had submitted samples of slag for analysis to regular geological laboratories and the results had been ambiguous. They indicated work 'with iron and copper'. Duncan with a doctorate in archaeology, as well as one in metallurgy, understood the importance of establishing whether this unique method of smelting without the use of clay was limited to copper or iron or both.

He showed convincingly that the metal produced at the site was copper, smelted from a malachite ore obtained from a nearby source at Swartmodder. Together we published a scholarly paper about "Smelting without Ceramics: the Drierivier Copper Smelting Site near Rehoboth, Namibia." I thought that the exciting discoveries we described ought to have made the headlines in the newspapers. But, sadly, this was another instance of valuable achievements going almost unnoticed!

While all this work was going on Namibia had become independent on 21 March 1990 and we had received funds from the German Government for the building of exhibition halls, a workshop, storerooms, a laboratory, offices and accommodation for the Rehoboth Museum. The community celebrated this news with an event which centred on starting with the digging up of the trenches for the foundations.

Skeletal iron silicate crystals called fayalite, embedded in dark glass. This is part of the slag waste associated with the copper production at Drierivier. The 0.03mm thick slide is viewed in the microscope under crossed polarized light, with a magnification of about 150 times. (Photo: Duncan Miller)

Copper slag, the waste material from production of copper by smelting malachite ore. The golden needles are fayalite, an iron silicate, embedded in a dark glass, with a scattering of small black crystals of copper. This slide is as thin as a sheet of paper, viewed under the microscope with crossed polarized light. The magnification is about 180 times. (Photo: Duncan Miller)

The money had been made available on condition that no new buildings were going to be erected. However, additions to existing buildings were permissible. Consequently Robert had designed three extensive wings to be added on to the residence of the Postmaster around a large courtyard. All our needs were comfortably accommodated in this complex, which was built in the style of the old house.

The community celebrated the extension of the museum building by starting to dig up the trenches for the foundation

The fourth Rehoboth Museum Seminar was held in one of the two large display halls before the roof had been put up and the fifth anniversary of the museum was held in the building before the walls had been plastered and painted. All these events were marked by a certain euphoria, which I ascribed to Independence. Regularly high ranking dignitaries were invited as Guests of Honour to Rehoboth Museum celebrations. Every new initiative was greeted with enthusiasm. The imagination of the Project Trust volunteers was end-less and welcomed by one and all. They persuaded members from different ethnic groups to construct examples of traditional houses on the grounds of the museum. This was a wonderful open-air exhibit and advertisement for the institution. They set up a service called 'museum on wheels' whereby they would hitch rides to farm schools. Armed with a box of display materials they told learners in the remote rural areas about the work of the museum.

Every school was encouraged to identify a site, which the school would adopt, observe, preserve, study and describe. The school at Kanobib under the headmanship of Reverend Stanley chose a wild fig tree growing out of a huge granite boulder. It was an icon for the small settlement. A year later a delightful exhibit had been put up at the school displaying all the parts of the tree and telling stories about the tree, which old residents had shared with the children. In 1992 the Museums Association of Namibia (MAN) established imme-diately after Independence, decided to improve on the 'museum on wheels' by organizing a national Mobile Museum Service.

Great strides had been made in terms of developing the Rehoboth Museum, this unique institution in a rural area of Namibia. The most momentous achievement was its estab-lishment of a Research Centre making it the only museum in the country with such a facility, apart from the state funded National Museum in Windhoek. More and more univer-sity students, researchers, scientists and scholars were attracted to the Museum. So Professor Trevor Jenkins from Wits introduced participants of a Rehoboth Museum Seminar to Mitochondrial Eve. According to the study of mitochondrial DNA the world's population now could be traced back to one woman living in Africa 150,000 yrs ago.

Other visitors undertook studies in Ethno-botany, Social Anthropology, History, Archaeol-ogy, Geology, and Ecology and in a wide range of multidisciplinary fields. Could this not develop into the kind of university we had been talking about at TUCSIN?

Dr Hartmut Lang and his wife Dr Cornelia Limpricht were spending a full year at the museum doing research on the history of the Basters and on the effects of farming on the natural surrounding. Their presence was an invaluable enrichment for the young institu-tion. The unstinting assistance of Cornelia and Hartmut was critical and made it possible to have the two new display halls of the museum ready for a grand inauguration in 1996. The Minister of Basic Education and Culture was the Guest of Honour at this auspicious occasion.

Ironically every success that was achieved at the museum generated a heavier load of problems in terms of more work, greater responsibilities, threats and dangers. We had started charging entrance fees and had established a small museum shop. This did gen-erate badly needed income but also required that money had to be accounted for. Propos-als for assistance were being granted more readily as the work of the museum became known. This meant money coming in for tasks that had to be administered and more money that had to be accounted for.

A serious blow to the development of the museum was the government's decision to withdraw its concession of accommodating the Project Trust volunteers at the school hostel. This meant that the museum had to terminate its contract with the organization because it was impossible to raise the funds for board, lodging and pocket money required in terms of our agreement with Project Trust.

An arrangement with the American based organization Earthwatch constituted another source of support for the museum and enabled me to continue with the archaeological fieldwork for a few more years. Groups of between one and ten Earthwatch volunteers would come to the museum for two to three weeks at a time to carry out carefully prepared programmes of fieldwork, anthropological research; designing and setting up of exhibits and public relations work such as manning a stand at the annual Rehoboth Show.

In the courtyard of the Rehoboth museum

The launch of a book, entitled 'A concise history of the Rehoboth Baster' written by Rudi Britz and Drs Hartmut Lang and Cornelia Limpricht with an appendix on the laws of the Rehoboth Baster by Dr Lang and Adolf Denk. The book was published in three languages.

The first team to come out undertook to reconstruct the excavation of the Drierivier cairn site. This open-air exhibit was representative of the seven excavated graves along the banks of the Oanob River. These prehistoric burials shared many important features, implying that funeral ceremonies had hardly changed over a period of some two hundred years. Presumably a stable community had inhabited the area for that time period, during the 17th and the 18th century. The fact that we had never found any copper products in these graves begged the question of whether the persons formally buried here two to three hundred years ago were the ones operating the copper smelting process. If not they, who did and what was the relationship between them?

We felt that it was appropriate to erect some kind of striking monument dedicated to this piece of history which we had literally unearthed here. Consequently Robert designed a partially sub-terranean concrete structure resembling a mini-amphitheatre or a huge cake from which a slice had been removed so that one could look at the content of the cake. A low brick wall enclosed three quarters of the original cairn. The numbers we had painted on the rocks before moving them and the plots we had drawn on graph paper while excavating, were invaluable in this reconstruction. The 'entrance' to the underground part of the structure consisted of semi-circular steps leading down to the exact place where the skeleton had been found. The section showing the excavated layers and the grave shaft were painted on the walls. This open-air exhibit became another hallmark of the Rehoboth Museum and many school children learned a great deal when we took them on excursions to the site.

The excavation of the eastern cairn at Drierivier was reconstructed in the form of an open air exhibit

Earthwatch teams comprised an amazing resource of specialised skills. These could have been exploited to immense benefit of the museum, had it been possible to obtain qualified personnel working at the museum on a permanent basis. That would have made it possible to carry out many of the wonderful suggestions Earthwatchers had made and which they would have loved to implement had there but been enough time.

All along I had been confident that sooner or later a local person would pitch up who would be committed enough to take over from me as curator of the museum. Since its inception I had spared no effort in keeping the Board of Curators informed about the developments at the Museum. Monthly reports were circulated and Board meetings were convened frequently. Wherever possible Board members were involved in the multitude of events that kept on coming up. They enthusiastically met and entertained visitors from all over the world. Invariably the guests were delighted.

A local teacher who was transferred from the Oanob Primary School to work at the museum kept saying that the work at the museum had developed her personality and strengthened her self-confidence like no other previous life experience. Unfortunately the backlog in her formal education and a health problem prevented her from shouldering the responsibilities that had to be taken on.

Volunteers and help from outside had only temporarily obscured the critical aspect of finding suitably qualified people locally to run the museum. My enchantment with Independence and my perceived notions about restoring people's pride in their history, their land, education and the contribution that the museum was making started to wear thin. There was no political will in recognising, let alone promoting, the work we were doing. What will happen when you retire one day? This was a question, which many people asked – including myself! TUCSIN, I thought and said, was soundly established and would be a back-up for the museum. Once I withdrew from the daily activities of TUCSIN I would be able to devote myself fully to the museum. The Board of the museum had supported my suggestion of identifying Vera Tune as my successor. Vera was a qualified schoolteacher, married to a successful medical doctor.

At one point we had managed to have her temporarily seconded to the museum and I had been impressed by her competence. She had also been chosen to become chairperson of the Board of Curators. I understood that her domestic situation of bringing up three little children and social obligations made great demands on her time. But, she would reassure me, that once the children were a bit bigger she would again be spending more time at the museum. I visualised her there on a full time permanent basis with me showing her the ropes. In that way I would gain time for catching up on a backlog of cataloguing and of writing up fieldwork. Yes, Vera would have to learn a great deal, but I felt that she had the potential. To expedite the learning process Dr Cornelia Limpricht had facilitated an exchange programme for Vera with a German museum.

At the same time professionalism and continuity in managing the sound operation of the museum should be ensured. When a well-qualified restorer of antique cultural artefacts offered to restore some of the items in our collection, the idea of a very practical project came up. Milly Möller designed a two-year training course for local people who would undergo in-service training under Milly's supervision and at the same time they would offer a service, which would generate an income. If things went well old furniture might be bought up, renovated and then sold again. Since every one seemed so taken up with this idea a trial run was implemented almost immediately. It fell victim to in-fighting and poor personnel and personal relations.

Among the requests of students and scientists to come to the museum for their studies there also were enquiries for work opportunities and offers for assistance by well-qualified persons. This led to contact with an organization called the Senior Expert Service and while Vera was at the Museum in Einbeck, Germany, we met Dr Martin Berger who had agreed to come and spend half a year at the museum.

We took Rehoboth school children on nature walks and Martin's knowledge, experience and personality made these excursions unforgettable. He also was an outstanding photographer and we recorded the rock art in the vicinity of Rehoboth in excellent, enlarged photographs, mounted and ready to be shown in an impressive exhibition. The curators learned a great deal simply by being in Dr Berger's company and listening to informal talks he gave on his speciality: the study of birds.

I told him about my limited contact with birds in terms of scientific research via the owls and their pellets which we had found at Mirabib. He promptly embarked on a study of owl pellets collected at the house of Leslie Maasdorp, the treasurer of the Board of Curators of the Rehoboth Museum an at a few other places in central Namibia. This work led to the publication of an 'Illustrated Key of the skulls of Central Namibian Small Mammal Species' by Martin Berger and Henning Vierhaus. This delightful little document represented the final constructive contribution the members of the Rehoboth Museum Board of Curators were able to affect before they were forced out of the office.

A conundrum of ill-advised decisions allowed the Bastergemeente of Rehoboth to claim total and exclusive control of the Rehoboth Museum. The Board of Curators was worn down and frustrated and eventually abdicated in 2002. All ties to me and to TUCSIN were severed. There had been a great deal of underhand plotting ranging from forging of signatures and defamation of character to the expropriation of my personal library, reprint collection and items given on loan for temporary exhibits. Perhaps an emerging sense of social pride is the most benevolent way of explaining this bitter phase at the end of twenty years of working towards the establishment of the Rehoboth Museum.

In spite of the disappointments it pleases me to look back at the achievements, the exciting experiences and the lessons that enriched my life. I remain archaeologically yours, Beatrice Sandelowsky.

Illustrated key of the skulls
of Central Namibian small mammal species

by Martin Berger and Henning Vierhaus

Striped Mouse, *Rhabdomys pumilio*
From: Schreber 1792

SELECTED BIBLIOGRAPHY

Brain, C.K. 1974 The use of microfaunal remains as habitat indicators in the Namib. S.Afr. Archaeol. Soc. Goodwin Ser. 2: 55-60.

Britz, R.G.; Lang, H. & Limpricht, C. 1999 A CONCISE HISTORY OF THE REHOBOTH BASTERS UNTIL 1990. Klaus Hess Publishers, Windhoek.

Bleek W.H.I. & Lucy Lloyd 1911 SPECIMENS OF BUSHMEN FOLKLORE. London, George Allen & Unwin, Ltd. (reprinted by C.Struik (Pty.) Ltd., Cape Town, 1968) and by Daimon Verlag, Einsiedeln, Switzerland, 2001. Pages 376-379.

Clark, J.D. 1970 THE PREHISTORY OF AFRICA. Thames & Hudson.

Greenberg, J.H. 1963 LANGUAGES OF AFRICA. Bloomington, Indiana.

Guthrie, M. 1968-9 COMPARATIVE BANTU, INTRODUCTION TO COMPARTIVE LINGUISTICS AND PREHISTORY OF THE BANTU LANGUAGE. 4 vols. London and California.

Miller, D. & Sandelowsky, B. H. 1999 Smelting without Ceramics: The Drierivier Copper Smelting Site near Rehoboth, Namibia. S. Afri. Archaeol. Bull. 54: 28 - 37.

Pachai, B. 1972 THE EARLY HISTORY OF MALAWI. Longman Group.

Pager, H. 1989 THE ROCK PAINTINGS OF THE UPPER BRANDBERG. Part I: AMIS GORGE. Africa Praehistorica 1. Köln.

Richter, J. 1991 STUDIEN ZUR URGESCHICHTE NAMIBIAS. HOLOZÄNE STRATIGRAPHIEN IM UMKREIS DES BRANDBERGES . Africa Praehistorica 3 , Köln.

Robinson, K. R. & Sandelowsky, B. H. 1969 The Iron Age of Northern Malawi: Recent Work. Azania, 3.

Sandelowsky, B.H. 1976 (a) The Beginning of Archaeo-ethno-botany in the Namib. In Palaeo-ecology of Africa, the Surrounding Islands & Antarctica. Ed. E. M. van Zinderen Bakker Sr.IX Balkema, Cape Town.

-do.-   1976 (b) Functional & Tourist Art along the Okavango River. In ETHNIC AND TOURIST ARTS. Ed. N.H.H. Graburn, University of California Press, Berkeley & Los Angeles.

-do.-   1977 MIRABIB, AN ARCHAEOLOGICAL STUDY IN THE NAMIB. In Madoqua Vol.10, No. 4 Journal of Nature Conservation & Desert Research, S.W.A.

-do.-   1979 Kapako and Vungu Vungu: Iron Age sites on the Kavango River. In van der Merwe, N. J. & Huffman, T.N. : Iron Age Studies in Southern Africa. Goodwin Series No. 3 S. Afri. Archaeol. Society.

-do. -   1983 (a) Is the Idea of a University for Namibia viable? Newsletter Vol. 7 No. 2. Basler Afrika Bibliographien.

-do.-   1983 (b) Archaeology in Namibia. American Scientist. Vol. 71.

-do.-   1990 A Multipurpose Plant of the Namib Desert in Southwestern Africa. In Biology & Utilization of the Cucurbitaeceae. Ed. Bates,D. M., Robinson, R. W. & Jeffrey, C. Cornell University Press. Ithaca & London.

-do.-   & Robinson, K. R. 1968 (a) Fingira. Preliminary Report. Malawi. Department of Antiquities Publ. No 3.

-do.-   & Pendleton, W. C. 1969 Stone Tuyères from South West Africa. S.Afri. Archaeol. Bull. 24 part 1.

-do.-   1970 Fieldwork at Meob Bay. In Namib & Meer, 1. Band, Heft 1. Museum Swakopmund.

-do.-   Scholz, H. & Ahlert, K. 1976 Ancient Tracks near Tsondap Vlei. Madoqua Vol. 9 No. 3 :57-58. Journal of Nature Conservation & Desert Research, S.W.A.

Shackley, M. 1980 An Acheulian industry with *Elephas recki* fauna from Namib IV, South West Africa, Namibia. In Nature 284: 340-341.

Scherz, E.R. 1970 FELSBILDER IN SÜDWEST-AFRIKA. Böhlau Verlag - Köln Wien.

Wendt, W.E. 1976 "Art mobîlier" from the Apollo 11 cave, South West Africa: Africa's oldest dated works of art. In S.Afr. Archaeol. Bull. 35: 5-11.

SELECTED INDEX

Saarbrücken University of 171
SADF (South African Defence Force) 164
Salvadore bush 148
Sambiu 77, 88
San 26, 65, 83, 86, 89, 94, 99
Sandwich Harbour 47
Scherz, Dr Ernst & Anneliese 157
Schliemann, Heinrich 40
Schmockel, Wolf 160
Scholz, Hans 41, 110, 111, 119, 159, 173
Schülein, Fritz 53
Seely, Mary 65, 105, 107, 112, 129, 133
Seeis133, 157
segments 23, 24
skelm 38
slag 26, 64, 67, 95
Small, Adam and Rosi 174
Sossus Vlei 44, 113, 121, 138
Sotho 105
Sout Rivier 124
South African Archaeological Bulletin 6
specularite 62
Spencer Bay 48
St Michael's College 161
Stanley, Reverend 190
State Museum 41
Steyn, M T Theunie 153, 173
Steyn, Dr Wilhelm 5, 6, 35, 102, 162
Steyn, Yvonne 173, 175
Strandlopers 44
Stuttgart 136
Striostrea margaritacea 110
Swakopmund 40
Swakop River 153
Swartz, Jackson 161
Sydow 37, 43, 82

Tamarix 115
Tankard, Tony 108, 109
tennis baan 61
theodolite 65
Terfezia pheilii 181
Tide Water Minerals 43
Tjijorakisa, Dr Siegfried 159
Tobias, Jerry 170, 172
Tobias, Phillip 117
Topnaar 113, 124
torch 54
Transvaal Museum 5, 137
trek 77

Troy 40
tsamma 131
Tsams Vlei 115
Tsondab Vlei 113, 119, 138
Tswana 105
TUCSIN (The University Centre for Studies
In Namibia) 157, 158, 171, 173, 177
Tune, Vera 193
tuyères 26, 36, 37, 41 - 43, 59, 64, 73, 182

UNIN (United Nations Institute for Namibia)
173
United Nations Organisation 40
University of the Western Cape (UWC)
102, 103, 153, 182
Uri Hauchab 48
Utuseb (formerly Ituseb) 173

Van Wyk, Andrew 179
Van Zeist 152
veld 38
veldkos 39, 89
Verwoerd, Hendrik 17, 35
vetlywe 62
Viereck, Albert 43, 82
Voigt, Elizabeth 53
Vorster, Balthasar 18, 35
Vungu Vungu 88, 89, 100

Wadley, Lynn 128
Walter, Professor and Erna Walter 136
Walvis Bay 44, 107, 108, 111, 138
watu 80
Weber, Dr Alfons 36, 110
Weber, Karin 155
Wendt, Dr Erich 65
Wenner method 184
Wilkinson, Justin 153
Windhoek 35
Wits (University of the Witwatersrand)
1, 102, 110
Würm 111

Xhosa 105
Yellen, John 2

Zambia 50
Zimbabwe 24
Zululand 16
Zygophyllum stapffii 115

SOUTHERN AFRICA

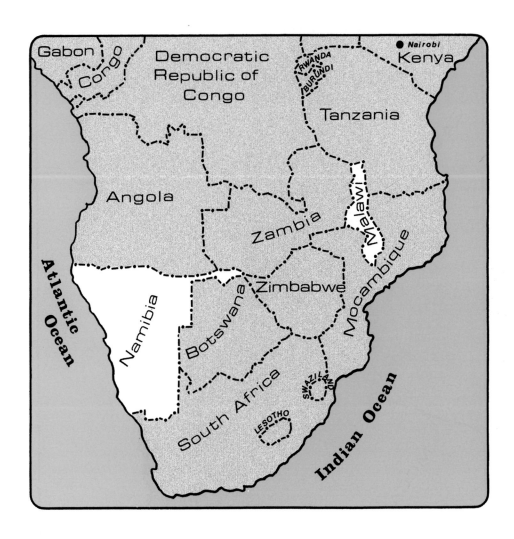

MALAWI

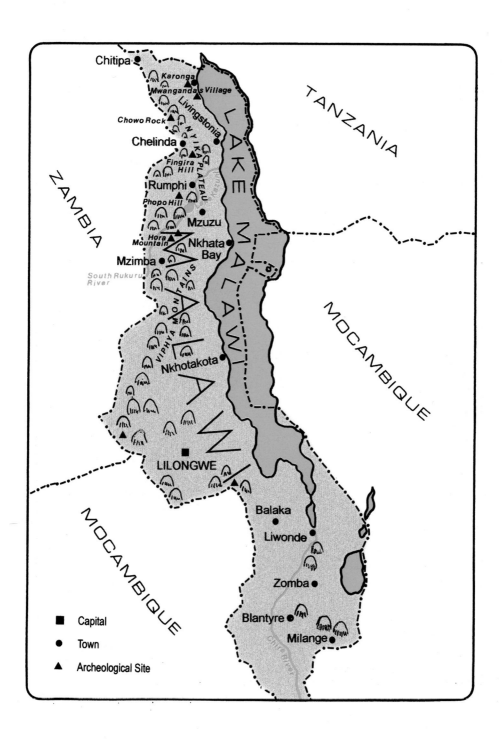